Life Lessons

from THE INSPIRED WORD of GOD

BOOK of JOHN

MAX LUCADO

General Editor

TABLE OF CONTENTS

HOW TO STUDY THE BIBLE

BY MAX LUCADO

This is a peculiar book you are holding. Words crafted in another language. Deeds done in a distant era. Events recorded in a far-off land. Counsel offered to a foreign people. This is a peculiar book.

It's surprising that anyone reads it. It's too old. Some of its writings date back five thousand years. It's too bizarre. The book speaks of incredible floods, fires, earthquakes, and people with supernatural abilities. It's too radical. The Bible calls for undying devotion to a carpenter who called himself God's Son.

Logic says this book shouldn't survive. Too old, too bizarre, too radical.

The Bible has been banned, burned, scoffed, and ridiculed. Scholars have mocked it as foolish. Kings have branded it as illegal. A thousand times over it the grave has been dug and the dirge has begun, but somehow the Bible never stays in the grave. Not only has it survived, it has thrived. It is the single most popular book in all of history. It has been the best-selling book in the world for years!

There is no way on earth to explain it. Which perhaps is the only explanation. The answer? The Bible's durability is not found on earth; it is found in heaven. For the millions who have tested its claims and claimed its promises, there is but one answer—the Bible is God's book and God's voice.

As you read it, you would be wise to give some thought to two questions. What is the purpose of the Bible? and How do I study the Bible? Time spent reflecting on these two issues will greatly enhance your Bible study.

What is the purpose of the Bible?

Let the Bible itself answer that question.

Since you were a child you have known the Holy Scriptures which are able to make you wise. And that wisdom leads to salvation through faith in Christ Jesus.

(2 Tim. 3:15)

The purpose of the Bible? Salvation. God's highest passion is to get his children home. His book, the Bible, describes his plan of salvation. The purpose of the Bible is to proclaim God's plan and passion to save his children.

That is the reason this book has endured through the centuries. It dares to tackle the toughest questions about life: Where do I go after I die? Is there a God? What do I do with my fears? The Bible offers answers to these crucial questions. It is the treasure map that leads us to God's highest treasure, eternal life.

But how do we use the Bible? Countless copies of Scripture sit unread on bookshelves and nightstands simply because people don't know how to read it. What can we do to make the Bible real in our lives?

The clearest answer is found in the words of Jesus.

"Ask," he promised, *"and God will give it to you. Search and you will find. Knock, and the door will open for you."*

(Matt. 7:7)

The first step in understanding the Bible is asking God to help us. We should read prayerfully. If anyone understands God's Word, it is because of God and not the reader.

But the Helper will teach you everything and will cause you to remember all that I told you. The Helper is the Holy Spirit whom the Father will send in my name.

(John 14:24)

Before reading the Bible, pray. Invite God to speak to you. Don't go to Scripture looking for your idea, go searching for his.

Not only should we read the Bible prayerfully, we should read it carefully. *Search and you will find* is the pledge. The Bible is not a newspaper to be skimmed but rather a mine to be quarried. *Search for it like silver, and hunt for it like hidden treasure. Then you will understand respect for the LORD, and you will find that you know God* (Prov. 2:4).

Any worthy find requires effort. The Bible is no exception. To understand the Bible you don't have to be brilliant, but you must be willing to roll up your sleeves and search.

Be a worker who is not ashamed and who uses the true teaching in the right way.

(2 Tim. 2:15)

Here's a practical point. Study the Bible a bit at a time. Hunger is not satisfied by eating twenty-one meals in one sitting once a week. The body needs a steady diet to remain strong. So does the soul. When God sent food to his people in the wilderness, he didn't provide loaves already made. Instead, he sent them manna in the shape of *thin flakes, like frost . . . on the desert ground* (Exod. 16:14).

God gave manna in limited portions.

God sends spiritual food the same way. He opens the heavens with just enough nutrients for today's hunger. He provides, *a command here, a command there. A rule here, a rule there. A little lesson here, a little lesson there* (Isa. 28:10).

Don't be discouraged if your reading reaps a small harvest. Some days a lesser portion is all that is needed. What is important is to search every day for that day's message. A steady diet of God's Word over a lifetime builds a healthy soul and mind.

A little girl returned from her first day at school. Her mom asked, "Did you learn anything?" "Apparently not enough," the girl responded, "I have to go back tomorrow and the next day and the next. . . ."

Such is the case with learning. And such is the case with Bible study. Understanding comes little by little over a lifetime.

There is a third step in understanding the Bible. After the asking and seeking comes the knocking. After you ask and search, then knock.

Knock, and the door will open for you.
(Matt. 7:7)

To knock is to stand at God's door. To make yourself available. To climb the steps, cross the porch, stand at the doorway, and volunteer. Knocking goes beyond the realm of thinking and into the realm of acting.

To knock is to ask, What can I do? How can I obey? Where can I go?

It's one thing to know what to do. It's another to do it. But for those who do it, those who choose to obey, a special reward awaits them.

The truly happy are those who carefully study God's perfect law that makes people free, and they continue to study it. They do not forget what they heard, but they obey what God's teaching says. Those who do this will be made happy.

(James 1:25)

What a promise. Happiness comes to those who do what they read! It's the same with medicine. If you only read the label but ignore the pills, it won't help. It's the same with food. If you only read the recipe but never cook, you won't be fed. And it's the same with the Bible. If you only read the words but never obey, you'll never know the joy God has promised.

Ask. Search. Knock. Simple, isn't it? Why don't you give it a try? If you do, you'll see why you are holding the most remarkable book in history.

JOHN

INTRODUCTION

*H*e's an old man, this one who sits on the stool and leans against the wall. Eyes closed and face soft, were it not for his hand stroking his beard, you'd think he was asleep.

Some in the room assume he is. He does this often during worship. As the people sing, his eyes will close and his chin will fall until it rests on his chest, and there he will remain motionless. Silent.

Those who know him well know better. They know he is not resting. He is traveling. Atop the music he journeys back, back, back until he is young again. Strong again. There again. There on the seashore with James and the apostles. There on the trail with the disciples and the women. There in the Temple with Caiaphas and the accusers.

It's been sixty years, but John sees him still. The decades took John's strength, but they didn't take his memory. The years dulled his sight, but they didn't dull his vision. The seasons may have wrinkled his face, but they didn't soften his love.

He had been with God. God had been with him. How could he forget?

❧ The wine that moments before had been water—John could still taste it.

❧ The mud placed on the eyes of the blind man in Jerusalem—John could still remember it.

❧ The aroma of Mary's perfume as it filled the room—John could still smell it.

And the voice. Oh, the voice. His voice. John could still hear it.

I am the light of the world, it rang . . . I am the door . . . I am the way, the truth, the life.

I will come back, it promised, and take you to be with me.

Those who believe in me, it assured, will have life even if they die.

John could hear him. John could see him. Scenes branded on his heart. Words seared into his soul. John would never forget. How could he? He had been there.

He opens his eyes and blinks. The singing has stopped. The teaching has begun. John looks at the listeners and listens to the teacher.

If only you could have been there, he thinks.

But he wasn't. Most weren't. Most weren't even born. And most who were there are dead. Peter is. So is James. Nathaniel, Martha, Bartholomew. They are all gone. Even Paul, the apostle who came late, is dead.

Only John remains.

He looks again at the church. Small but earnest. They lean forward to hear the teacher. John listens to him. What a task. Speaking of one he never saw. Explaining words he never heard. John is there if the teacher needs him.

But what will happen when John is gone?

What will the teacher do then? When John's voice is silent and his tongue stilled? Who will tell them how Jesus silenced the waves? Will they hear how he fed the thousands? Will they remember how he prayed for unity?

How will they know? If only they could have been there.

Suddenly, in his heart he knows what to do.

Later, under the light of a sunlit shaft, the old fisherman unfolds the scroll and begins to write the story of his life . . .

In the beginning was the Word . . .

LESSON ONE

WHEN GOD BECAME MAN

REFLECTION

Begin your study by sharing thoughts on this question.

1. Christ was born on earth of the will of God. When we accept him as Savior, we too are born (for a second time) of the will of God. Describe some of the events surrounding your second birth.

_____

_____

_____

BIBLE READING

Read John 1:1–18 from the NCV or the NKJV.

NCV

¹In the beginning there was the Word. The Word was with God, and the Word was God. ²He was with God in the beginning. ³All things were made by him, and nothing was made without him. ⁴In him there was life, and that life was the light of all people. ⁵The Light shines in the darkness, and the darkness has not overpowered it.

⁶There was a man named John who was sent by God. ⁷He came to tell people the truth about the Light so that through him all people could

NKJV

¹In the beginning was the Word, and the Word was with God, and the Word was God. ²He was in the beginning with God. ³All things were made through Him, and without Him nothing was made that was made. ⁴In Him was life, and the life was the light of men. ⁵And the light shines in the darkness, and the darkness did not comprehend it.

⁶There was a man sent from God, whose name was John. ⁷This man came for a witness, to bear witness of the Light, that all through

hear about the Light and believe. [8]John was not the Light, but he came to tell people the truth about the Light. [9]The true Light that gives light to all was coming into the world!

[10]The Word was in the world, and the world was made by him, but the world did not know him. [11]He came to the world that was his own, but his own people did not accept him. [12]But to all who did accept him and believe in him he gave the right to become children of God. [13]They did not become his children in any human way—by any human parents or human desire. They were born of God.

[14]The Word became a human and lived among us. We saw his glory—the glory that belongs to the only Son of the Father—and he was full of grace and truth. [15]John tells the truth about him and cries out, saying, "This is the One I told you about: 'The One who comes after me is greater than I am, because he was living before me.' "

[16]Because he was full of grace and truth, from him we all received one gift after another. [17]The law was given through Moses, but grace and truth came through Jesus Christ. [18]No one has ever seen God. But God the only Son is very close to the Father, and he has shown us what God is like.

him might believe. [8]He was not that Light, but was sent to bear witness of that Light. [9]That was the true Light which gives light to every man coming into the world.

[10]He was in the world, and the world was made through Him, and the world did not know Him. [11]He came to His own, and His own did not receive Him. [12]But as many as received Him, to them He gave the right to become children of God, to those who believe in His name: [13]who were born, not of blood, nor of the will of the flesh, nor of the will of man, but of God.

[14]And the Word became flesh and dwelt among us, and we beheld His glory, the glory as of the only begotten of the Father, full of grace and truth.

[15]John bore witness of Him and cried out, saying, "This was He of whom I said, 'He who comes after me is preferred before me, for He was before me.' "

[16]And of His fullness we have all received, and grace for grace. [17]For the law was given through Moses, but grace and truth came through Jesus Christ.

[18]No one has seen God at any time. The only begotten Son, who is in the bosom of the Father, He has declared Him.

DISCOVERY

Explore the Bible reading by discussing these questions.

2. In what way was Jesus' birth and life unique?

_____

_____

_____

3. What does this passage reveal about Jesus' mission?

_____

_____

_____

4. What does Jesus' life as a man tell us about God as Father?

_____

_____

_____

5. Jesus brought grace and truth to us. How does this benefit your life?

_____

_____

_____

6. Many people did not believe that Jesus was God's Son. What did they miss by not receiving him?

_____

_____

_____

INSPIRATION

Here is an uplifting thought from the *Inspirational Study Bible.*

It all happened in a moment, a most remarkable moment.

As moments go, that one appeared no different than any other. If you could somehow pick it up off the timeline and examine it, it would look exactly like the ones that have passed while you have read these words. It came and it went. It was preceded and succeeded by others just like it. It was one of the countless moments that have marked time since eternity became measurable.

But in reality, that particular moment was like none other. For through that segment of time a spectacular thing occurred. God became a man. While the creatures of earth walked unaware, Divinity arrived. Heaven opened herself and placed her most precious one in a human womb.

The omnipotent, in one instant, made himself breakable. He who had been spirit became pierceable. He who was larger than the universe became an embryo. And he who sustains the world with a word chose to be dependent upon the nourishment of a young girl.

God as a fetus. Holiness sleeping in a womb. The creator of life being created.

God was given eyebrows, elbows, two kidneys, and a spleen. He stretched against the walls and floated in the amniotic fluids of his mother.

God had come near.

He came, not as a flash of light or as an unapproachable conqueror, but as one whose first cries were heard by a peasant girl and a sleepy carpenter. The hands that first held him were unmanicured, calloused, and dirty.

No silk. No ivory. No hype. No party. No hoopla.

Were it not for the shepherds, there would have been no reception. And were it not for a group of star-gazers, there would have been no gifts.

Angels watched as Mary changed God's diaper. The universe watched with wonder as The Almighty learned to walk. Children played in the street with him. And had the synagogue leader in Nazareth known who was listening to his sermons. . . .

For thirty-three years he would feel everything you and I have ever felt. He felt weak. He grew weary. He was afraid of failure. He was susceptible to wooing women. He got colds, burped, and had body odor. His feelings got hurt. His feet got tired. And his head ached.

To think of Jesus in such a light is—well, it seems almost irreverent, doesn't it? It's not something we like to do; it's uncomfortable. It is much easier to keep the humanity out of the incarnation. Clean the manure from around the manger. Wipe the sweat out of his eyes. Pretend he never snored or blew his nose or hit his thumb with a hammer.

He's easier to stomach that way. There is something about keeping him divine that keeps him distant, packaged, predictable.

But don't do it. For heaven's sake, don't. Let him be as human as he intended to be. Let him into the mire and muck of our world. For only if we let him in can he pull us out.

(from *God Came Near*
by Max Lucado)

RESPONSE

Use these questions to share more deeply with each other.

7. What surprises you about Jesus coming to earth as a human being?

_____

_____

_____

8. What is comforting or encouraging about God taking on a human form?

_____

_____

_____

9. In what way does this truth inspire you?

_____

_____

_____

PRAYER

Blessed Lord and God, we come to you, thankful that you have pierced our world. You became flesh, you dwelled among us, you saw us in our fallen state, you reached in and pulled us out. You offered us salvation, you offered us mercy. We thank you for what you have done for us.

JOURNALING

Take a few moments to record your personal insights from this lesson.

How does the Light of God shine in my life each day?

ADDITIONAL QUESTIONS

10. What does Jesus' willingness to become a human being reveal about his heart?

_____

_____

_____

11. In what ways would your life be different if Jesus had not yet come to earth?

_____

_____

_____

12. How can I be a witness to others of the Light of Christ?

_____

_____

_____

For more Bible passages about God becoming a man, see John 14:6, 7;
1 Corinthians 8:5, 6; Galatians 4:4; Philippians 2:7, 8; Colossians 1: 15–20;
1 Timothy 3:16; Hebrews 2:14; 1 John 1:1, 2; 4:2.

To complete the book of John during this twelve-part study, read John 1:1–34.

LESSON TWO

A WEDDING IN CANA

REFLECTION

Begin your study by sharing thoughts on this question.

1. Think of the most memorable wedding you have attended. What made it so memorable?

_____

_____

_____

BIBLE READING

Read John 2:1–11 from the NCV or the NKJV.

NCV

¹Two days later there was a wedding in the town of Cana in Galilee. Jesus' mother was there, ²and Jesus and his followers were also invited to the wedding. ³When all the wine was gone, Jesus' mother said to him, "They have no more wine."

⁴Jesus answered, "Dear woman, why come to me? My time has not yet come."

⁵His mother said to the servants, "Do whatever he tells you to do."

⁶In that place there were six stone water jars that the Jews used in their washing ceremony.

NKJV

¹On the third day there was a wedding in Cana of Galilee, and the mother of Jesus was there. ²Now both Jesus and His disciples were invited to the wedding. ³And when they ran out of wine, the mother of Jesus said to Him, "They have no wine."

⁴Jesus said to her, "Woman, what does your concern have to do with Me? My hour has not yet come."

⁵His mother said to the servants, "Whatever He says to you, do it."

⁶Now there were set there six waterpots of

NCV

Each jar held about twenty or thirty gallons.

⁷Jesus said to the servants, "Fill the jars with water." So they filled the jars to the top.

⁸Then he said to them, "Now take some out and give it to the master of the feast."

So they took the water to the master. ⁹When he tasted it, the water had become wine. He did not know where the wine came from, but the servants who had brought the water knew. The master of the wedding called the bridegroom ¹⁰and said to him, "People always serve the best wine first. Later, after the guests have been drinking awhile, they serve the cheaper wine. But you have saved the best wine till now."

¹¹So in Cana of Galilee Jesus did his first miracle. There he showed his glory, and his followers believed in him.

NKJV

stone, according to the manner of purification of the Jews, containing twenty or thirty gallons apiece. ⁷Jesus said to them, "Fill the waterpots with water." And they filled them up to the brim. ⁸And He said to them, "Draw some out now, and take it to the master of the feast." And they took it. ⁹When the master of the feast had tasted the water that was made wine, and did not know where it came from (but the servants who had drawn the water knew), the master of the feast called the bridegroom. ¹⁰And he said to him, "Every man at the beginning sets out the good wine, and when the guests have well drunk, then the inferior. You have kept the good wine until now!"

¹¹This beginning of signs Jesus did in Cana of Galilee, and manifested His glory; and His disciples believed in Him.

DISCOVERY

Explore the Bible reading by discussing these questions.

2. Does it seem unusual to you that Jesus would attend a wedding? Why or why not?

_____

_____

_____

3. Why do you think Jesus chose to attend this wedding?

_____

_____

_____

4. For whose benefit did Jesus do this miracle?

_____

_____

_____

5. What characteristic of Jesus did this miracle reveal?

_____

_____

_____

6. How did this miracle affect the lives of the people around Jesus?

_____

_____

_____

INSPIRATION

Here is an uplifting thought from the *Inspirational Study Bible.*

Picture six men walking on a narrow road. . . .

The men's faces are eager, but common. Their leader is confident, but unknown. They call him Rabbi; he looks more like a laborer.

And well he should, for he's spent far more time building than teaching. But this week the teaching has begun.

Where are they going? To the temple to

worship? To the synagogue to teach? To the hills to pray? They haven't been told, but they each have their own idea.

John and Andrew expect to be led into the desert. That's where their previous teacher had taken them. John the Baptist would guide them into the barren hills and for hours they would pray. . . .

Surely he will do the same. . . .

Peter has another opinion. Peter is a man of action. A roll-up-your-sleeves kind of guy. A stand-up-and-say-it sort of fellow. He likes the idea of going somewhere. God's people need to be on the move. *Probably taking us somewhere to preach,* he is thinking to himself. And as they walk, Peter is outlining his own sermon, should Jesus need a breather.

Nathaniel would disagree. *Come and see,* his friend Philip had invited. So he came. And Nathaniel liked what he saw. In Jesus he saw a man of deep thought. A man of meditation . . . Nathaniel was convinced that Jesus was taking them to a place to ponder . . .

Did such speculation occur? Who knows? . . .

Maybe it was Andrew who asked it . . . .

"So Rabbi, where are you taking us? To the desert?"

"No," opines another, "he's taking us to the temple." . . .

Then a chorus of confusion breaks out and ends only when Jesus lifts his hand and says softly, "We're on our way to a wedding." . . .

"Why would we go to a wedding?"

Good question. Why would Jesus, on his first journey, take his followers to a party? Didn't they have work to do? Didn't he have principles to teach? Wasn't his time limited? How could a wedding fit with his purpose on earth?

Why did Jesus go to the wedding?

The answer? It's found in the second verse of John 2. "Jesus and his followers were also invited to the wedding." . . .

Big deal? I think so. I think it's significant that common folk in a little town enjoyed being with Jesus. I think it's noteworthy that the Almighty didn't act high and mighty. The Holy One wasn't holier-than-thou. The One who knew it all wasn't a know-it-all. The One who made the stars didn't keep his head in them. The One who owns all the stuff of earth never strutted it. . . .

Jesus was a likable fellow. And his disciples should be the same. I'm not talking debauchery, drunkenness, and adultery. I'm not endorsing compromise, coarseness, or obscenity. I am simply crusading for the freedom to enjoy a good joke, enliven a dull party, and appreciate a fun evening. . . .

We used to be good at it. What has happened to us? What happened to clean joy and loud laughter? Is it our neckties that choke us? Is it our diplomas that dignify us? Is it the pew that stiffens us?

. . . I must confess: it's been awhile since I've been accused of having too much fun. How about you?

(from *When God Whispers Your Name*
by Max Lucado)

RESPONSE

Use these questions to share more deeply with each other.

7. Have you ever seen God provide in a miraculous way? Explain.

_____

_____

_____

8. What prevents us from acknowledging God's provisions?

_____

_____

_____

9. List some ways God has met your needs. How does remembering God's provision in the past encourage you to trust him with your present needs?

_____

_____

_____

PRAYER

Lord Jesus, teach us to appreciate the simple pleasures in life and to enjoy the company of other people. May you walk with us, sharing life's pure pleasures and letting your light fall on life's common way.

JOURNALING

Take a few moments to record your personal insights from this lesson.

What reasons do I have to celebrate?

ADDITIONAL QUESTIONS

10. What simple pleasures bring you a sense of joy or fulfillment?

_____

_____

_____

11. What sometimes holds you back from enjoying life? Why?

_____

_____

_____

12. How do you think your Christian witness is affected when you don't take time to enjoy life?

_____

_____

_____

For more Bible passages on enjoying life, see Deuteronomy 6:1, 2; Psalm 91:15, 16; Ecclesiastes 2:24–26; 3:22; 11:8–10; Romans 15:13; Ephesians 6:1–3; 1 Timothy 6:17.

To complete the book of John during this twelve-part study, read John 1:35–2:25.

ADDITIONAL THOUGHTS

LESSON THREE

THE WOMAN AT THE WELL

REFLECTION

Begin your study by sharing thoughts on this question.

1. Share with your group the story of your conversion. How did your life change when you accepted Christ as your Savior?

BIBLE READING

Read John 4:5–30 from the NCV or the NKJV.

NCV

⁵In Samaria Jesus came to the town called Sychar, which is near the field Jacob gave to his son Joseph. ⁶Jacob's well was there. Jesus was tired from his long trip, so he sat down beside the well. It was about twelve o'clock noon. ⁷When a Samaritan woman came to the well to get some water, Jesus said to her, "Please give me a drink." ⁸(This happened while Jesus' followers were in town buying some food.)

⁹The woman said, "I am surprised that you

NKJV

⁵So He came to a city of Samaria which is called Sychar, near the plot of ground that Jacob gave to his son Joseph. ⁶Now Jacob's well was there. Jesus therefore, being wearied from His journey, sat thus by the well. It was about the sixth hour.

⁷A woman of Samaria came to draw water. Jesus said to her, "Give Me a drink." ⁸For His disciples had gone away into the city to buy food.

⁹Then the woman of Samaria said to Him,

ask me for a drink, since you are a Jewish man and I am a Samaritan woman." (Jewish people are not friends with Samaritans.)

[10]Jesus said, "If you only knew the free gift of God and who it is that is asking you for water, you would have asked him, and he would have given you living water."

[11]The woman said, "Sir, where will you get this living water? The well is very deep, and you have nothing to get water with. [12]Are you greater than Jacob, our father, who gave us this well and drank from it himself along with his sons and flocks?"

[13]Jesus answered, "Everyone who drinks this water will be thirsty again, [14]but whoever drinks the water I give will never be thirsty. The water I give will become a spring of water gushing up inside that person, giving eternal life."

[15]The woman said to him, "Sir, give me this water so I will never be thirsty again and will not have to come back here to get more water."

[16]Jesus told her, "Go get your husband and come back here."

[17]The woman answered, "I have no husband."

Jesus said to her, "You are right to say you have no husband. [18]Really you have had five husbands, and the man you live with now is not your husband. You told the truth."

[19]The woman said, "Sir, I can see that you are a prophet. [20]Our ancestors worshiped on this mountain, but you Jews say that Jerusalem is the place where people must worship."

[21]Jesus said, "Believe me, woman. The time is coming when neither in Jerusalem nor on this mountain will you actually worship the

"How is it that You, being a Jew, ask a drink from me, a Samaritan woman?" For Jews have no dealings with Samaritans.

[10]Jesus answered and said to her, "If you knew the gift of God, and who it is who says to you, 'Give Me a drink,' you would have asked Him, and He would have given you living water."

[11]The woman said to Him, "Sir, You have nothing to draw with, and the well is deep. Where then do You get that living water? [12]Are You greater than our father Jacob, who gave us the well, and drank from it himself, as well as his sons and his livestock?"

[13]Jesus answered and said to her, "Whoever drinks of this water will thirst again, [14]but whoever drinks of the water that I shall give him will never thirst. But the water that I shall give him will become in him a fountain of water springing up into everlasting life."

[15]The woman said to Him, "Sir, give me this water, that I may not thirst, nor come here to draw."

[16]Jesus said to her, "Go, call your husband, and come here."

[17]The woman answered and said, "I have no husband."

Jesus said to her, "You have well said, 'I have no husband,' [18]for you have had five husbands, and the one whom you now have is not your husband; in that you spoke truly."

[19]The woman said to Him, "Sir, I perceive that You are a prophet. [20]Our fathers worshiped on this mountain, and you Jews say that in Jerusalem is the place where one ought to worship."

NCV

Father. ²²You Samaritans worship something you don't understand. We understand what we worship, because salvation comes from the Jews. ²³The time is coming when the true worshipers will worship the Father in spirit and truth, and that time is here already. You see, the Father too is actively seeking such people to worship him. ²⁴God is spirit, and those who worship him must worship in spirit and truth."

²⁵The woman said, "I know that the Messiah is coming." (Messiah is the One called Christ.) "When the Messiah comes, he will explain everything to us."

²⁶Then Jesus said, "I am he—I, the one talking to you."

²⁷Just then his followers came back from town and were surprised to see him talking with a woman. But none of them asked, "What do you want?" or "Why are you talking with her?"

²⁸Then the woman left her water jar and went back to town. She said to the people, ²⁹"Come and see a man who told me everything I ever did. Do you think he might be the Christ?" ³⁰So the people left the town and went to see Jesus.

NKJV

²¹Jesus said to her, "Woman, believe Me, the hour is coming when you will neither on this mountain, nor in Jerusalem, worship the Father. ²²You worship what you do not know; we know what we worship, for salvation is of the Jews. ²³But the hour is coming, and now is, when the true worshipers will worship the Father in spirit and truth; for the Father is seeking such to worship Him. ²⁴God is Spirit, and those who worship Him must worship in spirit and truth."

²⁵The woman said to Him, "I know that Messiah is coming" (who is called Christ). "When He comes, He will tell us all things."

²⁶Jesus said to her, "I who speak to you am He."

²⁷And at this point His disciples came, and they marveled that He talked with a woman; yet no one said, "What do You seek?" or, "Why are You talking with her?"

²⁸The woman then left her waterpot, went her way into the city, and said to the men, ²⁹"Come, see a Man who told me all things that I ever did. Could this be the Christ?" ³⁰Then they went out of the city and came to Him.

DISCOVERY

Explore the Bible reading by discussing these questions.

2. What can you conclude about this woman's character?

_____

_____

_____

3. How do you think the woman felt when Jesus talked to her?

_____

_____

_____

4. How did Jesus demonstrate his love for this woman?

_____

_____

_____

5. How did the woman react to her encounter with Jesus?

_____

_____

_____

6. What do the woman's actions reveal about the way Jesus affected her life?

_____

_____

_____

INSPIRATION

Here is an uplifting thought from the *Inspirational Study Bible.*

Remarkable. Jesus didn't reveal the secret to King Herod. He didn't request an audience of the Sanhedrin and tell them the news. It wasn't within the colonnades of a Roman court that he announced his identity.

No, it was in the shade of a well in a rejected land to an ostracized woman. His eyes must have danced as he whispered the secret.

"I am the Messiah."

The most important phrase in the chapter is one easily overlooked. "Then, leaving her water jar, the woman went back to the town and said to the people, 'Come, see a man who told me everything I ever did. Could this be the Christ?'"

Don't miss the drama of the moment. Look at her eyes, wide with amazement. Listen to her as she struggles for words. "Y-y-y-you a-a-a-are the M-m-m-messiah!" And watch as she scrambles to her feet, takes one last look at this grinning Nazarene, turns and runs right into the burly chest of Peter. She almost falls, regains her balance, and hotfoots it toward her hometown.

Did you notice what she forgot? She forgot her water jar. She left behind the jug that had

caused the sag in her shoulders. She left behind the burden she brought.

Suddenly the shame of the tattered romances disappeared. Suddenly the insignificance of her life was swallowed by the significance of the moment. "God is here! God has come! God cares . . . for me!"

That is why she forgot her water jar. That is why she ran to the city. That is why she grabbed the first person she saw and announced her discovery, "I just talked to a man who knows everything I ever did . . . and he loves me anyway!"

The disciples offered Jesus some food. He refused it—he was too excited! He had just done what he does best. He had taken a life that was drifting and given it direction.

He was exuberant!

"Look!" he announced to the disciples, pointing at the woman who was running to the village. "Vast fields of human souls are ripening all around us, and are ready now for the reaping."

(from *Six Hours One Friday* by Max Lucado)

RESPONSE

Use these questions to share more deeply with each other.

7. In what ways can you identify with the woman in this story?

_____

_____

_____

8. What does this story reveal about God's attitude toward sinful people?

_____

_____

_____

9. When have you felt God's concern and love for you?

_____

_____

_____

PRAYER

Father, your Word assures us that no one is beyond hope. You accept and love each one of us, in spite of our failures. You offer us salvation. You offer us mercy. You offer us love. Thank you for intervening in our lives and rescuing us from the bondage of sin. We praise you for your mercy, forgiveness, and love.

JOURNALING

Take a few moments to record your personal insights from this lesson.

How can I reach out to others like Jesus did?

ADDITIONAL QUESTIONS

10. What keeps you from showing God's love to others?

_____

_____

_____

11. How does the woman's response to Jesus inspire you?

_____

_____

_____

12. How do Jesus' actions in this story encourage you to treat others?

_____

_____

_____

For more Bible passages on God's mercy and love for sinners, see Exodus 34:6; Deuteronomy 4:31; Luke 1:50; 19:1–10; John 3:16; 8:3–11; Ephesians 2:1–6.

To complete the book of John during this twelve-part study, read John 3:1–4:42.

LESSON FOUR

HEALING THE SICK

REFLECTION

Begin your study by sharing thoughts on this question.

1. Think of a time when a friend showed special concern for you during a difficult time in your life. How did that person's support help you?

_____

_____

BIBLE READING

Read John 5:1–15 from the NCV or the NKJV.

NCV

¹Later Jesus went to Jerusalem for a special Jewish feast. ²In Jerusalem there is a pool with five covered porches, which is called Bethzatha in the Jewish language. This pool is near the Sheep Gate. ³Many sick people were lying on the porches beside the pool. Some were blind, some were crippled, and some were paralyzed. ⁵A man was lying there who had been sick for thirty-eight years. ⁶When Jesus saw the man and knew that he had been sick for such a long time, Jesus asked him, "Do you want to be well?"

⁷The sick man answered, "Sir, there is no one to help me get into the pool when the water

NKJV

¹After this there was a feast of the Jews, and Jesus went up to Jerusalem. ²Now there is in Jerusalem by the Sheep Gate a pool, which is called in Hebrew, Bethesda, having five porches. ³In these lay a great multitude of sick people, blind, lame, paralyzed, waiting for the moving of the water. ⁴For an angel went down at a certain time into the pool and stirred up the water; then whoever stepped in first, after the stirring of the water, was made well of whatever disease he had. ⁵Now a certain man was there who had an infirmity thirty-eight years. ⁶When Jesus saw him lying there, and knew that he already had been in that

NCV

starts moving. While I am coming to the water, someone else always gets in before me."

⁸Then Jesus said, "Stand up. Pick up your mat and walk." ⁹And immediately the man was well; he picked up his mat and began to walk.

The day this happened was a Sabbath day. ¹⁰So the Jews said to the man who had been healed, "Today is the Sabbath. It is against our law for you to carry your mat on the Sabbath day."

¹¹But he answered, "The man who made me well told me, 'Pick up your mat and walk.'"

¹²Then they asked him, "Who is the man who told you to pick up your mat and walk?"

¹³But the man who had been healed did not know who it was, because there were many people in that place, and Jesus had left.

¹⁴Later, Jesus found the man at the Temple and said to him, "See, you are well now. Stop sinning so that something worse does not happen to you."

¹⁵Then the man left and told the Jews that Jesus was the one who had made him well.

NKJV

condition a long time, He said to him, "Do you want to be made well?"

⁷The sick man answered Him, "Sir, I have no man to put me into the pool when the water is stirred up; but while I am coming, another steps down before me."

⁸Jesus said to him, "Rise, take up your bed and walk." ⁹And immediately the man was made well, took up his bed, and walked.

And that day was the Sabbath. ¹⁰The Jews therefore said to him who was cured, "It is the Sabbath; it is not lawful for you to carry your bed."

¹¹He answered them, "He who made me well said to me, 'Take up your bed and walk.' "

¹²Then they asked him, "Who is the Man who said to you, 'Take up your bed and walk'?"

¹³But the one who was healed did not know who it was, for Jesus had withdrawn, a multitude being in that place. ¹⁴Afterward Jesus found him in the temple, and said to him, "See, you have been made well. Sin no more, lest a worse thing come upon you."

¹⁵The man departed and told the Jews that it was Jesus who had made him well.

DISCOVERY

Explore the Bible reading by discussing these questions.

2. What do you think motivated Jesus to go to Bethesda (also called Bethzatha) during a time of celebration?

_____

_____

3. This story focuses on one invalid man at Bethzatha. What words would you use to describe this man's life?

_____

_____

_____

4. Why do you think Jesus chose to help this particular man?

_____

_____

_____

5. After healing the man, why was it important to Jesus to find him and speak to him again?

_____

_____

_____

6. What do Jesus' actions in this story teach us about his character?

_____

_____

_____

INSPIRATION

Here is an uplifting thought from the *Inspirational Study Bible.*

It's called Bethesda. It could be called Central Park, Metropolitan Hospital, or even Joe's Bar and Grill. It could be the homeless hud-dled beneath a downtown overpass. It could be Calvary Baptist. It could be any collection of hurting people.

An underwater spring caused the pool to bubble occasionally. The people believed the bubbles were caused by the dipping of angels' wings. They also believed that the first person to touch the water after the angel did would be healed. Did healing occur? I don't know. But I do know crowds of invalids came to give it a try.

Picture a battleground strewn with wounded bodies, and you see Bethesda. Imagine a nursing home overcrowded and understaffed, and you see the pool. Call to mind the orphans in Bangladesh or the abandoned in New Delhi, and you will see what people saw when they passed Bethesda. As they passed, what did they hear? An endless wave of groans. What did they witness? A field of faceless need. What did they do? Most walked past, ignoring the people.

But not Jesus. He is in Jerusalem for a feast. . . .

He is alone. He is not there to teach the disciples or to draw a crowd. The people need him—so he's there.

Can you picture it? Jesus walking among the suffering.

What is he thinking? When an infected hand touches his ankle, what does he do? When a blind child stumbles in Jesus' path, does he reach down to catch the child? When a wrinkled hand extends for alms, how does Jesus respond?

Whether the watering hole is Bethesda or Bill's Bar . . . how does God feel when people hurt?

It's worth the telling of the story if all we do is watch him walk. It's worth it just to know he even came. He didn't have to, you know. Surely there are more sanitary crowds in Jerusalem. Surely there are more enjoyable activities. After all, this is the Passover feast. It's an exciting time in the holy city. People have come from miles around to meet God in the temple.

Little do they know that God is with the sick.

Little do they know that God is walking slowly, stepping carefully between the beggars and the blind.

Little do they know that the strong young carpenter who surveys the ragged landscape of pain is God.

(from *He Still Moves Stones*
by Max Lucado)

RESPONSE

Use these questions to share more deeply with each other.

7. How were others who witnessed this healing affected?

_____

_____

_____

8. What are some of the challenges of ministering to people with a serious illness? What are the rewards?

_____

_____

_____

9. How can we demonstrate God's love to people who are suffering?

_____

_____

_____

PRAYER

Forgive us, Father, for ignoring the needs of others. Help us respond to the suffering around us. Fill us with your love. Give us your compassion for the hurting, your love for the despised, your mercy for the afflicted.

JOURNALING

Take a few moments to record your personal insights from this lesson.

How have I felt God's love for me during painful times?

ADDITIONAL QUESTIONS

10. Why is it important for believers to minister to hurting people?

_____

_____

_____

11. Do you know someone who is hurting? How can you reach out to that person?

_____

_____

_____

12. How can we become more sensitive to the suffering of others?

_____

_____

_____

For more Bible passages about helping the needy, see Matthew 25:34–46;
1 Thessalonians 5:14; Hebrews 6:10, 11.

To complete the book of John during this twelve-part study, read John 4:43–5:47.

ADDITIONAL THOUGHTS

LESSON FIVE

A HUNGRY CROWD

REFLECTION

Begin your study by sharing thoughts on this question.

1. Think of a time when God provided for your needs in an unusual or surprising way. How did that experience strengthen your faith?

_____

_____

_____

BIBLE READING

Read John 6:1–15 from the NCV or the NKJV.

NCV

¹After this, Jesus went across Lake Galilee (or, Lake Tiberias). ²Many people followed him because they saw the miracles he did to heal the sick. ³Jesus went up on a hill and sat down there with his followers. ⁴It was almost the time for the Jewish Passover Feast.

⁵When Jesus looked up and saw a large crowd coming toward him, he said to Philip, "Where can we buy enough bread for all these people to eat?" ⁶(Jesus asked Philip this question to test him, because Jesus already knew what he planned to do.)

NKJV

¹After these things Jesus went over the Sea of Galilee, which is the Sea of Tiberias. ²Then a great multitude followed Him, because they saw His signs which He performed on those who were diseased. ³And Jesus went up on the mountain, and there He sat with His disciples.

⁴Now the Passover, a feast of the Jews, was near. ⁵Then Jesus lifted up His eyes, and seeing a great multitude coming toward Him, He said to Philip, "Where shall we buy bread, that these may eat?" ⁶But this He said to test him, for He Himself knew what He would do.

NCV

[7]Philip answered, "We would all have to work a month to buy enough bread for each person to have only a little piece."

[8]Another one of his followers, Andrew, Simon Peter's brother, said, [9]"Here is a boy with five loaves of barley bread and two little fish, but that is not enough for so many people."

[10]Jesus said, "Tell the people to sit down." This was a very grassy place, and about five thousand men sat down there. [11]Then Jesus took the loaves of bread, thanked God for them, and gave them to the people who were sitting there. He did the same with the fish, giving as much as the people wanted.

[12]When they had all had enough to eat, Jesus said to his followers, "Gather the leftover pieces of fish and bread so that nothing is wasted." [13]So they gathered up the pieces and filled twelve baskets with the pieces left from the five barley loaves.

[14]When the people saw this miracle that Jesus did, they said, "He must truly be the Prophet who is coming into the world."

[15]Jesus knew that the people planned to come and take him by force and make him their king, so he left and went into the hills alone.

NKJV

[7]Philip answered Him, "Two hundred denarii worth of bread is not sufficient for them, that every one of them may have a little."

[8]One of His disciples, Andrew, Simon Peter's brother, said to Him, [9]"There is a lad here who has five barley loaves and two small fish, but what are they among so many?"

[10]Then Jesus said, "Make the people sit down." Now there was much grass in the place. So the men sat down, in number about five thousand. [11]And Jesus took the loaves, and when He had given thanks He distributed them to the disciples, and the disciples to those sitting down; and likewise of the fish, as much as they wanted. [12]So when they were filled, He said to His disciples, "Gather up the fragments that remain, so that nothing is lost." [13]Therefore they gathered them up, and filled twelve baskets with the fragments of the five barley loaves which were left over by those who had eaten. [14]Then those men, when they had seen the sign that Jesus did, said, "This is truly the Prophet who is to come into the world."

[15]Therefore when Jesus perceived that they were about to come and take Him by force to make Him king, He departed again to the mountain by Himself alone.

DISCOVERY

Explore the Bible reading by discussing these questions.

2. Why do you think the people went out to see Jesus without bringing along any food?

_____

_____

3. Why did Jesus ask Philip how they could feed the crowd?

_____

_____

_____

4. What can we learn from Philip's response?

_____

_____

_____

5. What do you think Jesus wanted his disciples to learn from this event?

_____

_____

_____

6. Who are you most like in this story? Philip? Andrew? The boy? The people? Why?

_____

_____

_____

INSPIRATION

Here is an uplifting thought from the *Inspirational Study Bible.*

Interestingly, the stress seen that day is not on Jesus' face, but on the faces of the disciples. "Send the crowds away," they demand. Fair request. "After all," they are saying, "You've taught them. You've healed them. You've accommodated them. And now they're getting hungry. If we don't send them away, they'll want you to feed them, too!"

I wish I could have seen the expression on the disciples' faces when they heard the Master's response. . . .

"You give them something to eat." . . .

Rather than look to God, they looked in their wallets. "That would take eight months of a man's wages! Are we to go and spend that much on bread and give it to them to eat?"

"Y-y-y-you've got to be kidding."

"He can't be serious."

"It's one of Jesus' jokes."

"Do you know how many people are out there?"

Eyes watermelon wide. Jaws dangling open. One ear hearing the din of the crowd, the other the command of God.

Don't miss the contrasting views. When Jesus saw the people, he saw an opportunity to love and affirm value. When the disciples saw the people they saw thousands of problems.

Also, don't miss the irony. In the midst of a bakery—in the presence of the Eternal Baker—they tell the "Bread of Life" that there is no bread.

How silly we must appear to God.

Here's where Jesus should have given up. This is the point in the pressure-packed day where Jesus should have exploded. The sorrow, the life threats, the exuberance, the crowds, the interruptions, the demands, and now this. His own disciples can't do what he asks them. In front of five thousand men, they let him down.

"Beam me up, Father," should have been Jesus' next words. But they weren't. Instead he inquires, "How many loaves do you have?"

The disciples bring him a little boy's lunch. A lunch pail becomes a banquet, and all are fed. No word of reprimand is given. No furrowed brow of anger is seen. No "I-told-you-so" speech is delivered. The same compassion Jesus extends to the crowd is extended to his friends.

(from *In the Eye of the Storm* by Max Lucado)

RESPONSE

Use these questions to share more deeply with each other.

7. What problems in your life seem to have no solutions?

_____

_____

_____

8. Do you find it difficult to trust God to meet your needs? Why?

_____

_____

_____

9. What does this story teach us about the way God provides for his people?

_____

_____

_____

PRAYER

Father, why do we doubt you? Time and time again, you have proved your faithfulness, yet our faith falters. Thank you for continually providing for our needs. Keep us from doubt. Fill us with faith in you. Remind us that you are bigger than all of our problems and needs.

JOURNALING

Take a few moments to record your personal insights from this lesson.

What keeps me from trusting God to meet my needs?

ADDITIONAL QUESTIONS

10. In what ways has God given you wisdom and strength to overcome difficulties in your life?

_____

_____

_____

11. How does God want you to deal with your doubts?

_____

_____

_____

12. How does the faith of other believers inspire us to trust God?

_____

_____

_____

For more Bible passages on God's provision for his people, see Genesis 2:15, 16; Exodus 16:1–31; Psalm 20:7; Proverbs 3:5–10; Matthew 6:25–34.

To complete the book of John during this twelve-part study, read John 6:1–71.

ADDITIONAL THOUGHTS

LESSON SIX

A GUILTY WOMAN

REFLECTION

Begin your study by sharing thoughts on this question.

1. List some things that make you feel loved and accepted by others.

_____

_____

_____

BIBLE READING

Read John 8:1–11 from the NCV or the NKJV.

NCV

¹Jesus went to the Mount of Olives. ²But early in the morning he went back to the Temple, and all the people came to him, and he sat and taught them. ³The teachers of the law and the Pharisees brought a woman who had been caught in adultery. They forced her to stand before the people. ⁴They said to Jesus, "Teacher, this woman was caught having sexual relations with a man who is not her husband. ⁵The law of Moses commands that we stone to death every woman who does this. What do you say we should do?" ⁶They were asking this to trick

NKJV

¹But Jesus went to the Mount of Olives.
²Now early in the morning He came again into the temple, and all the people came to Him; and He sat down and taught them. ³Then the scribes and Pharisees brought to Him a woman caught in adultery. And when they had set her in the midst, ⁴they said to Him, "Teacher, this woman was caught in adultery, in the very act. ⁵Now Moses, in the law, commanded us that such should be stoned. But what do You say?" ⁶This they said, testing Him, that they might have something of which to accuse Him. But

NCV

Jesus so that they could have some charge against him.

But Jesus bent over and started writing on the ground with his finger. ⁷When they continued to ask Jesus their question, he raised up and said, "Anyone here who has never sinned can throw the first stone at her." ⁸Then Jesus bent over again and wrote on the ground.

⁹Those who heard Jesus began to leave one by one, first the older men and then the others. Jesus was left there alone with the woman standing before him. ¹⁰Jesus raised up again and asked her, "Woman, where are they? Has no one judged you guilty?"

¹¹She answered, "No one, sir."

Then Jesus said, "I also don't judge you guilty. You may go now, but don't sin anymore."

NKJV

Jesus stooped down and wrote on the ground with His finger, as though He did not hear.

⁷So when they continued asking Him, He raised Himself up and said to them, "He who is without sin among you, let him throw a stone at her first." ⁸And again He stooped down and wrote on the ground. ⁹Then those who heard it, being convicted by their conscience, went out one by one, beginning with the oldest even to the last. And Jesus was left alone, and the woman standing in the midst. ¹⁰When Jesus had raised Himself up and saw no one but the woman, He said to her, "Woman, where are those accusers of yours? Has no one condemned you?"

¹¹She said, "No one, Lord."

And Jesus said to her, "Neither do I condemn you; go and sin no more."

DISCOVERY

Explore the Bible reading by discussing these questions.

2. Why did the religious leaders bring the adulterous woman to Jesus?

_____

_____

_____

3. How was Jesus' attitude toward the woman different than the crowd's attitude?

_____

_____

_____

4. Why do you think the older men were the first to leave the scene?

_____

_____

_____

5. With which group or person in the story do you identify?

_____

_____

6. What words would you use to describe the way Jesus treated the guilty woman?

_____

_____

_____

INSPIRATION

Here's an uplifting thought from the *Inspirational Study Bible.*

Sightless and heartless redeemers. Redeemers without power. That's not the Redeemer of the New Testament.

Compare the blind Christ I saw in Rio to the compassionate one seen by a frightened woman early one morning in Jerusalem.

Jesus sits surrounded by a horseshoe of listeners. Some nod their heads in agreement and open their hearts in obedience. They have accepted the teacher as their teacher and are learning to accept him as their Lord.

We don't know his topic that morning. Prayer, perhaps. Or maybe kindness or anxiety. But whatever it was, it was soon interrupted when people burst into the courtyard.

Determined, they erupt out of a narrow street and stomp toward Jesus. The listeners scramble to get out of the way. The mob is made up of religious leaders, the elders and deacons of their day. Respected and important men. And struggling to keep her balance on the crest of this angry wave is a scantily-clad woman.

Only moments before she had been in bed with a man who was not her husband. Was this how she made her living? Maybe. Maybe not. We don't know.

But we do know that a door was jerked open and she was yanked from a bed. She barely had time to cover her body before she was dragged into the street by two men the age of her father.

And now, with holy strides, the mob storms toward the teacher. They throw the woman in his direction. She nearly falls.

"We found this woman in bed with a man!" cries the leader. "The law says to stone her. What do you say?"

In her despair she looks at the Teacher. His eyes don't glare. "Don't worry," they whisper, "it's okay." And for the first time that morning she sees kindness.

As Jesus looked at this daughter, did his mind race back? Did he relive the act of forming this child in heaven? Did he see her as he had originally made her?

So, with the tenderness only a father can have, he set out to untie the knots and repair the holes.

He begins by diverting the crowd's attention. He draws on the ground. Everybody looks down. The woman feels relief as the eyes of the men look away from her.

The accusers are persistent. "Tell us teacher! What do you want us to do with her?"

He just raised his head and offered an invitation, "I guess if you've never made a mistake, then you have a right to stone this woman." He looked back down and began to draw on the earth again.

Someone cleared his throat as if to speak, but no one spoke. Feet shuffled. Eyes dropped.

Then thud . . . thud . . . thud . . . rocks fell to the ground.

And they walked away. They came as one, but they left one by one.

Jesus told the woman to look up. "Is there no one to condemn you?"

Maybe she expected him to scold her. Perhaps she expected him to walk away from her. I'm not sure, but I do know this: What she got, she never expected. She got a promise and a commission.

The promise: "Then neither do I condemn you."

The commission: "Go and sin no more."

The woman turns and walks into anonymity. She's never seen or heard from again. But we can be confident of one thing: On that morning in Jerusalem, she saw Jesus and Jesus saw her. And could we somehow transport her to Rio de Janeiro and let her stand at the base of the *Cristo redentor*, I know what her response would be.

"That's not the Jesus I saw," she would say. For the Jesus she saw didn't have a hard heart. And the Jesus that saw her didn't have blind eyes.

However, if we could somehow transport her to Calvary and let her stand at the base of the cross . . . you know what she would say. "That's him."

She would recognize his voice. It's raspier and weaker, but the words are the same, "Father, forgive them. . . ." And she would recognize his eyes. How could she ever forget those eyes? Clear and tear-filled. Eyes that saw her not as she was, but as she was intended to be.

(from *Six Hours One Friday*
by Max Lucado)

RESPONSE

Use these questions to share more deeply with each other.

7. How does Jesus' interaction with this sinful woman encourage you?

_____

_____

_____

8. What was the attitude of the religious leaders toward the woman? Toward Jesus?

_____

_____

_____

9. How can we avoid these same attitudes?

_____

_____

_____

PRAYER

Father, you are compassionate and forgiving. Like the woman in this story, we stand amazed that you would have such mercy on us. We thank you for your unconditional love. We are not what we should be, but we accept your forgiveness and claim your salvation.

JOURNALING

Take a few moments to record your personal insights from this lesson.

For what sinful attitudes or actions do I need to ask God's forgiveness?

ADDITIONAL QUESTIONS

10. What does this passage reveal about God's view of sin?

_____

_____

_____

11. Why do you think we rank some sins as being far worse than others?

_____

_____

_____

12. How does this passage challenge your attitude about people caught in certain sins?

_____

_____

_____

For more Bible passages on God's forgiveness, see Exodus 34:6, 7; Deuteronomy 4:31; Luke 1:50; Acts 10:43; Ephesians 1:7; 2:4, 5; 1 John 1:8, 9.

To complete the book of John during this twelve-part study, read John 7:1–8:59.

ADDITIONAL THOUGHTS

LESSON SEVEN

A MAN BORN BLIND

REFLECTION

Begin your study by sharing thoughts on this question.

1. Think about your personal strengths and weaknesses. How has God worked through your weaknesses for his glory?

_____

_____

_____

BIBLE READING

Read John 9:1–12 from the NCV or the NKJV.

NCV

¹As Jesus was walking along, he saw a man who had been born blind. ²His followers asked him, "Teacher, whose sin caused this man to be born blind—his own sin or his parents' sin?"

³Jesus answered, "It is not this man's sin or his parents' sin that made him be blind. This man was born blind so that God's power could be shown in him. ⁴While it is daytime, we must continue doing the work of the One who sent

NKJV

¹Now as Jesus passed by, He saw a man who was blind from birth. ²And His disciples asked Him, saying, "Rabbi, who sinned, this man or his parents, that he was born blind?"

³Jesus answered, "Neither this man nor his parents sinned, but that the works of God should be revealed in him. ⁴I must work the works of Him who sent Me while it is day; the night is coming when no one can work. ⁵As

NCV

me. Night is coming, when no one can work. [5]While I am in the world, I am the light of the world."

[6]After Jesus said this, he spit on the ground and made some mud with it and put the mud on the man's eyes. [7]Then he told the man, "Go and wash in the Pool of Siloam." (Siloam means Sent.) So the man went, washed, and came back seeing.

[8]The neighbors and some people who had earlier seen this man begging said, "Isn't this the same man who used to sit and beg?"

[9]Some said, "He is the one," but others said, "No, he only looks like him."

The man himself said, "I am the man."

[10]They asked, "How did you get your sight?"

[11]He answered, "The man named Jesus made some mud and put it on my eyes. Then he told me to go to Siloam and wash. So I went and washed, and then I could see."

[12]They asked him, "Where is this man?"

"I don't know," he answered.

NKJV

long as I am in the world, I am the light of the world."

[6]When He had said these things, He spat on the ground and made clay with the saliva; and He anointed the eyes of the blind man with the clay. [7]And He said to him, "Go, wash in the pool of Siloam" (which is translated, Sent). So he went and washed, and came back seeing.

[8]Therefore the neighbors and those who previously had seen that he was blind said, "Is not this he who sat and begged?"

[9]Some said, "This is he." Others said, "He is like him."

He said, "I am he."

[10]Therefore they said to him, "How were your eyes opened?"

[11]He answered and said, "A Man called Jesus made clay and anointed my eyes and said to me, 'Go to the pool of Siloam and wash.' So I went and washed, and I received sight."

[12]Then they said to him, "Where is He?"

He said, "I do not know."

DISCOVERY

Explore the Bible reading by discussing these questions.

2. What assumptions did Jesus' followers make about this man's blindness?

_____

_____

_____

3. What misconception did Jesus correct?

_____

_____

_____

4. How did Jesus involve the blind man in the healing process?

_____

_____

_____

5. Why do you think Jesus sent the man to wash in a pool before he healed him?

_____

_____

_____

6. How did the people of the town respond to the miracle?

_____

_____

_____

INSPIRATION

Here is an uplifting thought from the *Inspirational Study Bible.*

Or what about the blind man Jesus and the disciples discovered?

The followers thought he was a great theological case study.

"Why do you think he's blind?" one asked.

"He must have sinned."

"No, it's his folks' fault."

"Jesus, what do you think? Why is he blind?"

"He's blind to show what God can do."

The apostles knew what was coming; they had seen this look in Jesus' eyes before. They knew what he was going to do, but they didn't know how he was going to do it. "Lightning? Thunder? A shout? A clap of the hands?" They all watched.

Jesus began to work his mouth a little. The onlookers stared. "What is he doing?" He moved his jaw as if he were chewing on something.

Some of the people began to get restless. Jesus just chewed. His jaw rotated around until he had what he wanted. Spit. Ordinary saliva.

If no one said it, somebody had to be thinking it: "Yuk!"

Jesus spat on the ground, stuck his finger into the puddle, and stirred. Soon it was a mud pie, and he smeared some of the mud across the blind man's eyes.

The same One who'd turned a stick into a scepter and a pebble into a missile now turned saliva and mud into a balm for the blind.

Once again, the mundane became majestic. Once again the dull became divine, the humdrum holy. Once again God's power was seen, not through the ability of the instrument, but through its availability.

"Blessed are the meek," Jesus explained. Blessed are the available. Blessed are the conduits, the tunnels, the tools. Deliriously joyful are the ones who believe that if God has used sticks, rocks, and spit to do his will, then he can use us.

(from *The Applause of Heaven* by Max Lucado)

RESPONSE

Use these questions to share more deeply with each other.

7. What can we learn from responses of the blind man and the townspeople to Jesus?

_____

_____

_____

8. If you had been one of the townspeople, how do you think you would have responded?

_____

_____

_____

9. When have you seen a person's weakness or disability used for God's glory?

_____

_____

_____

PRAYER

We pray, O Father, that you would increase our faith. Forgive us for doubting your ability to use us for your glory. Forgive us for demanding proof instead of simply believing in you. Use all that we have to accomplish your purposes.

JOURNALING

Take a few moments to record your personal insights from this lesson.

How can God use my weaknesses or problems for his glory?

ADDITIONAL QUESTIONS

10. What fresh insight have you gained from this passage about the struggles of life?

_____

_____

_____

11. How do you need to change your attitude toward your personal weaknesses and strengths?

_____

_____

_____

12. Why does God choose to use our weaknesses and problems to bring glory to himself?

_____

_____

_____

For more Bible passages on being used by God, see Exodus 3:7–4:12; Joshua 1:1–9; Romans 8:26; 1 Corinthians 1:26–28; 2 Corinthians 12:7–10; 2 Timothy 2:21.

To complete the book of John during this twelve-part study, read John 9:1–10:42.

ADDITIONAL THOUGHTS

LESSON EIGHT

THE LOSS OF A FRIEND

REFLECTION

Begin your study by sharing thoughts on this question.

1. Think of a time in your life when a bad experience turned out for good. How did that affect you?

_____

_____

_____

BIBLE READING

Read John 11:17–44 from the NCV or the NKJV.

NCV

¹⁷When Jesus arrived, he learned that Lazarus had already been dead and in the tomb for four days. ¹⁸Bethany was about two miles from Jerusalem. ¹⁹Many of the Jews had come there to comfort Martha and Mary about their brother.

²⁰When Martha heard that Jesus was coming, she went out to meet him, but Mary stayed home. ²¹Martha said to Jesus, "Lord, if you had been here, my brother would not have died.

NKJV

¹⁷So when Jesus came, He found that he had already been in the tomb four days. ¹⁸Now Bethany was near Jerusalem, about two miles away. ¹⁹And many of the Jews had joined the women around Martha and Mary, to comfort them concerning their brother.

²⁰Then Martha, as soon as she heard that Jesus was coming, went and met Him, but Mary was sitting in the house. ²¹Then Martha said to Jesus, "Lord, if You had been here, my brother

NCV

²²But I know that even now God will give you anything you ask."

²³Jesus said, "Your brother will rise and live again."

²⁴Martha answered, "I know that he will rise and live again in the resurrection on the last day."

²⁵Jesus said to her, "I am the resurrection and the life. Those who believe in me will have life even if they die. ²⁶And everyone who lives and believes in me will never die. Martha, do you believe this?"

²⁷Martha answered, "Yes, Lord. I believe that you are the Christ, the Son of God, the One coming to the world."

²⁸After Martha said this, she went back and talked to her sister Mary alone. Martha said, "The Teacher is here and he is asking for you." ²⁹When Mary heard this, she got up quickly and went to Jesus. ³⁰Jesus had not yet come into the town but was still at the place where Martha had met him. ³¹The Jews were with Mary in the house, comforting her. When they saw her stand and leave quickly, they followed her, thinking she was going to the tomb to cry there. ³²But Mary went to the place where Jesus was. When she saw him, she fell at his feet and said, "Lord, if you had been here, my brother would not have died."

³³When Jesus saw Mary crying and the Jews who came with her also crying, he was upset and was deeply troubled. ³⁴He asked, "Where did you bury him?" "Come and see, Lord," they said.

³⁵Jesus cried.

³⁶So the Jews said, "See how much he loved him."

NKJV

would not have died. ²²But even now I know that whatever You ask of God, God will give You."

²³Jesus said to her, "Your brother will rise again."

²⁴Martha said to Him, "I know that he will rise again in the resurrection at the last day."

²⁵Jesus said to her, "I am the resurrection and the life. He who believes in Me, though he may die, he shall live. ²⁶And whoever lives and believes in Me shall never die. Do you believe this?"

²⁷She said to Him, "Yes, Lord, I believe that You are the Christ, the Son of God, who is to come into the world."

²⁸And when she had said these things, she went her way and secretly called Mary her sister, saying, "The Teacher has come and is calling for you." ²⁹As soon as she heard that, she arose quickly and came to Him. ³⁰Now Jesus had not yet come into the town, but was in the place where Martha met Him. ³¹Then the Jews who were with her in the house, and comforting her, when they saw that Mary rose up quickly and went out, followed her, saying, "She is going to the tomb to weep there."

³²Then, when Mary came where Jesus was, and saw Him, she fell down at His feet, saying to Him, "Lord, if You had been here, my brother would not have died."

³³Therefore, when Jesus saw her weeping, and the Jews who came with her weeping, He groaned in the spirit and was troubled. ³⁴And He said, "Where have you laid him?"

They said to Him, "Lord, come and see."

³⁵Jesus wept. ³⁶Then the Jews said, "See how He loved him!"

NCV

[37]But some of them said, "If Jesus opened the eyes of the blind man, why couldn't he keep Lazarus from dying?"

[38]Again feeling very upset, Jesus came to the tomb. It was a cave with a large stone covering the entrance. [39]Jesus said, "Move the stone away."

Martha, the sister of the dead man, said, "But, Lord, it has been four days since he died. There will be a bad smell."

[40]Then Jesus said to her, "Didn't I tell you that if you believed you would see the glory of God?"

[41]So they moved the stone away from the entrance. Then Jesus looked up and said, "Father, I thank you that you heard me. [42]I know that you always hear me, but I said these things because of the people here around me. I want them to believe that you sent me." [43]After Jesus said this, he cried out in a loud voice, "Lazarus, come out!" [44]The dead man came out, his hands and feet wrapped with pieces of cloth, and a cloth around his face.

Jesus said to them, "Take the cloth off of him and let him go."

NKJV

[37]And some of them said, "Could not this Man, who opened the eyes of the blind, also have kept this man from dying?"

[38]Then Jesus, again groaning in Himself, came to the tomb. It was a cave, and a stone lay against it. [39]Jesus said, "Take away the stone."

Martha, the sister of him who was dead, said to Him, "Lord, by this time there is a stench, for he has been dead four days."

[40]Jesus said to her, "Did I not say to you that if you would believe you would see the glory of God?" [41]Then they took away the stone from the place where the dead man was lying. And Jesus lifted up His eyes and said, "Father, I thank You that You have heard Me. [42]And I know that You always hear Me, but because of the people who are standing by I said this, that they may believe that You sent Me." [43]Now when He had said these things, He cried with a loud voice, "Lazarus, come forth!" [44]And he who had died came out bound hand and foot with grave-clothes, and his face was wrapped with a cloth. Jesus said to them, "Loose him, and let him go."

DISCOVERY

Explore the Bible reading by discussing these questions.

2. How did Mary and Martha feel about Jesus' late arrival?

_____

_____

_____

3. How did Mary and Martha express their feelings?

_____

_____

_____

4. Do you think Jesus' words to Martha were reassuring to her? Why or why not?

_____

_____

_____

5. How did Martha communicate her belief in Jesus?

_____

_____

_____

6. How did Jesus respond to Mary, Martha, and the others' mourning?

_____

_____

_____

INSPIRATION

Here is an uplifting thought from the *Inspirational Study Bible.*

Have you been there? Have you been called to stand at the thin line that separates the living from the dead? Have you lain awake at night listening to machines pumping air in and out of your lungs? Have you watched sickness corrode and atrophy the body of a friend? Have you lingered behind at the cemetery long after the others have left, gazing in disbelief at the metal casket that contains the body that contained the soul of the one you can't believe is gone?

If so, then this canyon is not unfamiliar to you. You've heard the lonesome whistle of the winds. You've heard the painful questions. Why? What for? ricochet answerless off the canyon walls. And you've kicked loose rocks off the edge and listened for the sound of their crashing, which never comes. . . .

Standing on the edge of the canyon draws all of life into perspective. What matters and what doesn't are easily distinguished. Above the canyon wall no one is concerned about salaries or positions. No one asks about the car you drive or what part of town you live in. As aging humans stand beside this ageless chasm, all the games and disguises of life seem sadly silly. . . .

It is possible that I'm addressing someone who is walking the canyon wall. Someone you love dearly has been called into the unknown and you are alone. Alone with your fears and alone with your doubts. If this is the case, • please read the rest of this piece very carefully. Look carefully at the scene described in John 11.

In this scene there are two people: Martha and Jesus. And for all practical purposes they are the only two people in the universe.

Her words were full of despair. "If you had been here. . . ." She stares into the Master's face with confused eyes. She'd been strong long enough; now it hurt too badly. Lazarus was dead. Her brother was gone. And the one man who could have made a difference didn't. He hadn't even made it for the burial. Something about death makes us accuse God of betrayal. "If God were here there would be no death!" we claim.

You see, if God is God anywhere, he has to be God in the face of death. Pop psychology can deal with depression. Pep talks can deal with pessimism. Prosperity can handle hunger. But only God can deal with our ultimate dilemma—death. And only the God of the Bible has dared to stand on the canyon's edge and offer an answer. He has to be God in the face of death. If not, he is not God anywhere.

Jesus wasn't angry at Martha. Perhaps it was his patience that caused her to change her tone from frustration to earnestness. "Even now God will give you whatever you ask."

Jesus then made one of those claims that place him either on the throne or in the asylum: "Your brother will rise again."

Martha misunderstood. (Who wouldn't have?) "I know he will rise again in the resurrection at the last day."

That wasn't what Jesus meant. Don't miss the context of the next words. Imagine the setting: Jesus has intruded on the enemy's turf; he's standing in Satan's territory, Death Canyon. His stomach turns as he smells the sulfuric stench of the ex-angel, and he winces as he hears the oppressed wails of those trapped in the prison. Satan has been here. He has violated one of God's creations.

With his foot planted on the serpent's head, Jesus speaks loudly enough that his words echo off the canyon walls.

"I am the resurrection and the life. He who believes in me will live, even though he dies; and whoever lives and believes in me will never die" (John 11:25).

It is the hinge point in history. A chink has been found in death's armor. The keys to the halls of hell have been claimed. The buzzards scatter and the scorpions scurry as Life confronts death—and wins! The wind stops. A cloud blocks the sun and a bird chirps in the distance while a humiliated snake slithers between the rocks and disappears into the ground.

The stage has been set for a confrontation at Calvary.

But Jesus isn't through with Martha. With eyes locked on hers he asks the greatest question found in Scripture, a question meant as much for you and me as for Martha.

"Do you believe this?"

Wham! There it is. The bottom line. The dimension that separates Jesus from a thousand gurus and prophets who have come down the pike. The question that drives any responsible listener to absolute obedience or to total rejection of the Christian faith.

"Do you believe this?"

Let the question sink into your heart for a minute. Do you believe that a young, penniless itinerant is larger than your death? Do you truly believe that death is nothing more than an entrance ramp to a new highway?

"Do you believe this?"

Jesus didn't pose this query as a topic for discussion in Sunday schools. It was never intended to be dealt with while basking in the stained glass sunlight or while seated on padded pews.

No. This is a canyon question. A question which makes sense only during an all-night vigil or in the stillness of smoke-filled waiting rooms. A question that makes sense when all of our props, crutches, and costumes are taken away. For then we must face ourselves as we really are: rudderless humans tailspinning toward disaster. And we are forced to see him for what he claims to be: our only hope.

(from *God Came Near*
by Max Lucado)

RESPONSE

Use these questions to share more deeply with each other.

7. How did Martha's response demonstrate both faith and a lack of faith?

_____

_____

_____

8. How do Jesus' words and actions in this passage comfort you?

_____

_____

_____

9. Have you seen God use pain to draw a person closer to him? Explain.

_____

_____

_____

PRAYER

Father, thank you for caring about our pain and disappointments. Calm the whirling winds of fear and hurt that threaten our faith. Keep us from trying to cope with our struggles by our own strength and willpower. Help us to release our emotions to you and trust you to sustain us. Thank you for your comforting words of wisdom. Let us receive the healing of the Holy Spirit.

JOURNALING

Take a few moments to record your personal insights from this lesson.

How can I surrender past hurts and disappointments to God?

ADDITIONAL QUESTIONS

10. How has God helped you during a sad or disappointing time?

_____

_____

_____

11. Why is it important to let Christ help you through painful times?

_____

_____

_____

12. How can you share the pain of others who suffer?

_____

_____

_____

For more Bible passages dealing with hurts, see Matthew 9:36; 11:28–30; Romans 12:15; 2 Corinthians 1:3–7.

To complete the book of John during this twelve-part study, read John 11:1–12:50.

ADDITIONAL THOUGHTS

LESSON NINE

THE MASTER SERVANT

REFLECTION

Begin your study by sharing thoughts on this question.

1. Think of a special time when you enjoyed fellowship with other believers. Why did you enjoy it so much?

_____

_____

_____

BIBLE READING

Read John 13:1–20 from the NCV or the NKJV.

NCV

¹It was almost time for the Jewish Passover Feast. Jesus knew that it was time for him to leave this world and go back to the Father. He had always loved those who were his own in the world, and he loved them all the way to the end.

²Jesus and his followers were at the evening meal. The devil had already persuaded Judas Iscariot, the son of Simon, to turn against Jesus. ³Jesus knew that the Father had given him power over everything and that he had come

NKJV

¹Now before the feast of the Passover, when Jesus knew that His hour had come that He should depart from this world to the Father, having loved His own who were in the world, He loved them to the end.

²And supper being ended, the devil having already put it into the heart of Judas Iscariot, Simon's son, to betray Him, ³Jesus, knowing that the Father had given all things into His hands, and that He had come from God and

NCV

from God and was going back to God. ⁴So during the meal Jesus stood up and took off his outer clothing. Taking a towel, he wrapped it around his waist. ⁵Then he poured water into a bowl and began to wash the followers' feet, drying them with the towel that was wrapped around him.

⁶Jesus came to Simon Peter, who said to him, "Lord, are you going to wash my feet?"

⁷Jesus answered, "You don't understand now what I am doing, but you will understand later."

⁸Peter said, "No, you will never wash my feet." Jesus answered, "If I don't wash your feet, you are not one of my people."

⁹Simon Peter answered, "Lord, then wash not only my feet, but wash my hands and my head, too!"

¹⁰Jesus said, "After a person has had a bath, his whole body is clean. He needs only to wash his feet. And you men are clean, but not all of you." ¹¹Jesus knew who would turn against him, and that is why he said, "Not all of you are clean."

¹²When he had finished washing their feet, he put on his clothes and sat down again. He asked, "Do you understand what I have just done for you? ¹³You call me 'Teacher' and 'Lord,' and you are right, because that is what I am. ¹⁴If I, your Lord and Teacher, have washed your feet, you also should wash each other's feet. ¹⁵I did this as an example so that you should do as I have done for you. ¹⁶I tell you the truth, a servant is not greater than his master. A messenger is not greater than the one who sent him. ¹⁷If you know these things, you will be happy if you do them.

NKJV

was going to God, ⁴rose from supper and laid aside His garments, took a towel and girded Himself. ⁵After that, He poured water into a basin and began to wash the disciples' feet, and to wipe them with the towel with which He was girded. ⁶Then He came to Simon Peter. And Peter said to Him, "Lord, are You washing my feet?"

⁷Jesus answered and said to him, "What I am doing you do not understand now, but you will know after this."

⁸Peter said to Him, "You shall never wash my feet!"

Jesus answered him, "If I do not wash you, you have no part with Me."

⁹Simon Peter said to Him, "Lord, not my feet only, but also my hands and my head!"

¹⁰Jesus said to him, "He who is bathed needs only to wash his feet, but is completely clean; and you are clean, but not all of you." ¹¹For He knew who would betray Him; therefore He said, "You are not all clean."

¹²So when He had washed their feet, taken His garments, and sat down again, He said to them, "Do you know what I have done to you? ¹³You call me Teacher and Lord, and you say well, for so I am. ¹⁴If I then, your Lord and Teacher, have washed your feet, you also ought to wash one another's feet. ¹⁵For I have given you an example, that you should do as I have done to you. ¹⁶Most assuredly, I say to you, a servant is not greater than his master; nor is he who is sent greater than he who sent him. ¹⁷If you know these things, blessed are you if you do them.

¹⁸"I do not speak concerning all of you. I

NCV

[18]"I am not talking about all of you. I know those I have chosen. But this is to bring about what the Scripture said: 'The man who ate at my table has turned against me.' [19]I am telling you this now before it happens so that when it happens, you will believe that I am he. [20]I tell you the truth, whoever accepts anyone I send also accepts me. And whoever accepts me also accepts the One who sent me."

NKJV

know whom I have chosen; but that the Scripture may be fulfilled, 'He who eats bread with Me has lifted up his heel against Me.' [19]Now I tell you before it comes, that when it does come to pass, you may believe that I am He. [20]Most assuredly, I say to you, he who receives whomever I send receives Me; and he who receives Me receives Him who sent Me."

DISCOVERY

Explore the Bible reading by discussing these questions.

2. What do you suppose the atmosphere was like at this meal?

_____

_____

_____

3. What range of feelings did Jesus have for his disciples?

_____

_____

_____

4. How did Jesus show his love for his friends?

_____

_____

_____

5. What was Simon Peter's immediate reaction to being served by Jesus?

_____

_____

_____

6. Why was it difficult for Simon Peter to accept Jesus' service?

_____

_____

_____

INSPIRATION

Here is an uplifting thought from the *Inspirational Study Bible.*

What kind of life did those first Christians live? When they were together, they devoted themselves to four things. John Calvin wrote in his *Institutes*: "We must endeavor to keep and preserve this order, if we will be judged faithful to the church before God and the angels."

First, they gave themselves to "the apostles' teaching." That was everything the apostles had seen Jesus do and heard him say. Eventually they got it all written down; now we call it the New Testament. Our equivalent today of the "apostles' teaching" would be Bible study.

Second, they devoted themselves to the fellowship. That was simply being together for the joy of being together. Why draw your stimuli for life, they must have been thinking, from non-Christians who have nothing to contribute, when you could be absorbing more and more of the life of Christ from within your Christian friends? This was no deliberate cut-off from worldlings to be exclusive. Their fellowship was the strong base from which they reached out to others. But there was far more power for evangelism in this close-knit community than we find today—we, whose spirits are diluted by so much exposure to the world—even though we may say it's to win them for Christ!

Third, they devoted themselves to breaking bread together. I'm sure this meant Communion, but I think it meant other meals, too. . . .

Number four ingredient in their new life together: "the prayers." That's right, the Greek has the article *the* in front of it, and it's the same word as in Acts 3:1: "One day Peter and John were going up to the temple at the time of the prayers." In other words, "the prayers" were the stated times for worship at the temple, and all believers went together. . . .

No doubt a lot of former activities had to go, for the early Christians. They "eliminated" and they "concentrated"; they "continually devoted themselves" to these four things.

Friends, let's check our lifestyles. Have we eliminated a lot of clutter from our lives so that we, and the ones around us who want to go hard after God, can give ourselves to Bible study, to fellowship, to eating together, and to the regular services of the church?

(from *Discipling One Another* by Anne Ortlund)

RESPONSE

Use these questions to share more deeply with each other.

7. What long-term impact do you think Jesus' actions had on the disciples?

_____

_____

_____

8. When has the humble service of a fellow believer inspired you?

_____

_____

_____

9. What are some of the rewards of serving others?

_____

_____

_____

PRAYER

Father, in Jesus we see the perfect model of humble service. Help us to be like him. Open our eyes to the needs of others. Help us to follow your Word. Help us to follow in Christ's footsteps.

JOURNALING

Take a few moments to record your personal insights from this lesson.

What practical things can I do to serve others?

ADDITIONAL QUESTIONS

10. Why is it important for believers to have fellowship with each other?

_____

_____

_____

11. How does it affect you to see people serving with humility in the church?

_____

_____

_____

12. When have you found it difficult to accept help from a fellow believer? Why?

_____

_____

_____

For more Bible passages on serving, see Matthew 20:25–28; Ephesians 6:7; Galatians 5:13; Philippians 2:7.

To complete the book of John during this twelve-part study, read John 13:1–14:14.

LESSON TEN

JESUS' PRAYER

REFLECTION

Begin your study by sharing thoughts on this question.

1. Think of a recent answer to your prayer. How did God's answer show his faithfulness to you?

_____

_____

_____

BIBLE READING

Read John 17:1–26 from the NCV or the NKJV.

NCV

¹After Jesus said these things, he looked toward heaven and prayed, "Father, the time has come. Give glory to your Son so that the Son can give glory to you. ²You gave the Son power over all people so that the Son could give eternal life to all those you gave him. ³And this is eternal life: that people know you, the only true God, and that they know Jesus Christ, the One you sent. ⁴Having finished the work you gave me to do, I brought you glory on earth. ⁵And now, Father, give me glory with you; give me

NKJV

¹Jesus spoke these words, lifted up His eyes to heaven, and said: "Father, the hour has come. Glorify Your Son, that Your Son also may glorify You, ²as You have given Him authority over all flesh, that He should give eternal life to as many as You have given Him. ³And this is eternal life, that they may know You, the only true God, and Jesus Christ whom You have sent. ⁴I have glorified You on the earth. I have finished the work which You have given Me to do. ⁵And now, O Father, glorify Me together with

the glory I had with you before the world was made.

⁶"I showed what you are like to those you gave me from the world. They belonged to you, and you gave them to me, and they have obeyed your teaching. ⁷Now they know that everything you gave me comes from you. ⁸I gave them the teachings you gave me, and they accepted them. They knew that I truly came from you, and they believed that you sent me. ⁹I am praying for them. I am not praying for people in the world but for those you gave me, because they are yours. ¹⁰All I have is yours, and all you have is mine. And my glory is shown through them. ¹¹I am coming to you; I will not stay in the world any longer. But they are still in the world. Holy Father, keep them safe by the power of your name, the name you gave me, so that they will be one, just as you and I are one. ¹²While I was with them, I kept them safe by the power of your name, the name you gave me. I protected them, and only one of them, the one worthy of destruction, was lost so that the Scripture would come true.

¹³"I am coming to you now. But I pray these things while I am still in the world so that these followers can have all of my joy in them. ¹⁴I have given them your teaching. And the world has hated them, because they don't belong to the world, just as I don't belong to the world. ¹⁵I am not asking you to take them out of the world but to keep them safe from the Evil One. ¹⁶They don't belong to the world, just as I don't belong to the world. ¹⁷Make them ready for your service through your truth; your teaching is truth. ¹⁸I have sent them into the world, just as you

Yourself, with the glory which I had with You before the world was.

⁶"I have manifested Your name to the men whom You have given Me out of the world. They were Yours, You gave them to Me, and they have kept Your word. ⁷Now they have known that all things which You have given Me are from You. ⁸For I have given to them the words which You have given Me; and they have received them, and have known surely that I came forth from You; and they have believed that You sent Me.

⁹"I pray for them. I do not pray for the world but for those whom You have given Me, for they are Yours. ¹⁰And all Mine are Yours, and Yours are Mine, and I am glorified in them. ¹¹Now I am no longer in the world, but these are in the world, and I come to You. Holy Father, keep through Your name those whom You have given Me, that they may be one as We are. ¹²While I was with them in the world, I kept them in Your name. Those whom You gave Me I have kept; and none of them is lost except the son of perdition, that the Scripture might be fulfilled. ¹³But now I come to You, and these things I speak in the world, that they may have My joy fulfilled in themselves. ¹⁴I have given them Your word; and the world has hated them because they are not of the world, just as I am not of the world. ¹⁵I do not pray that You should take them out of the world, but that You should keep them from the evil one. ¹⁶They are not of the world, just as I am not of the world. ¹⁷Sanctify them by Your truth. Your word is truth. ¹⁸As You sent Me into the world, I also have sent them into the world. ¹⁹And for their sakes I sanctify Myself, that they also may be sanctified by the truth.

NCV

sent me into the world. [19]For their sake, I am making myself ready to serve so that they can be ready for their service of the truth.

[20]"I pray for these followers, but I am also praying for all those who will believe in me because of their teaching. [21]Father, I pray that they can be one. As you are in me and I am in you, I pray that they can also be one in us. Then the world will believe that you sent me. [22]I have given these people the glory that you gave me so that they can be one, just as you and I are one. [23]I will be in them and you will be in me so that they will be completely one. Then the world will know that you sent me and that you loved them just as much as you loved me.

[24]"Father, I want these people that you gave me to be with me where I am. I want them to see my glory, which you gave me because you loved me before the world was made. [25]Father, you are the One who is good. The world does not know you, but I know you, and these people know you sent me. [26]I showed them what you are like, and I will show them again. Then they will have the same love that you have for me, and I will live in them."

NKJV

[20]"I do not pray for these alone, but also for those who will believe in Me through their word; [21]that they all may be one, as You, Father, are in Me, and I in You; that they also may be one in Us, that the world may believe that You sent Me. [22]And the glory which You gave Me I have given them, that they may be one just as We are one: [23]I in them, and You in Me; that they may be made perfect in one, and that the world may know that You have sent Me, and have loved them as You have loved Me.

[24]"Father, I desire that they also whom You gave Me may be with Me where I am, that they may behold My glory which You have given Me; for You loved Me before the foundation of the world. [25]O righteous Father! The world has not known You, but I have known You; and these have known that You sent Me. [26]And I have declared to them Your name, and will declare it, that the love with which You loved Me may be in them, and I in them."

DISCOVERY

Explore the Bible reading by discussing these questions.

2. For whom did Jesus pray?

_____

_____

_____

3. How does this prayer depict Jesus' relationship with God the Father?

_____

_____

_____

4. What does Jesus desire for his followers?

_____

_____

_____

5. What spiritual battle is described in Jesus' prayer?

_____

_____

_____

6. How are believers equipped for this battle?

_____

_____

_____

INSPIRATION

Here is an uplifting thought from the *Inspirational Study Bible.*

Do we pray for God's will, or demand our own way? Prayer needs to be an integral part of our lives, so that when a crisis comes we have the strength and faith to pray for God's will. Someone said that strength in prayer is better than length in prayer. However, Martin Luther said, "I have so much to do today that I shall spend the first three hours in prayer."

Jesus frequently prayed alone, separating Himself from every earthly distraction. I would strongly urge you to select a place—a room or corner in your home, place of work, or in your yard or garden—where you can regularly meet God alone. . . .

When we see the need of someone else, pray. When we know someone is pain, pray. Let someone know you have prayed for them, and ask others to pray for you.

A missionary and his family were forced to camp outside on a hill. They had money with them and were fearful of an attack by roving thieves. After praying, they went to sleep. Months later an injured man was brought into the mission hospital. He asked the missionary if he had soldiers guarding him on that special night. "We intended to rob you," he said, "but we were afraid of the twenty-seven soldiers."

When the missionary returned to his homeland, he related this strange story, and a member of his church said, "We had a prayer meeting that night, and I took the roll. There were just twenty-seven of us present."

(from *Hope for the Troubled Heart*
by Billy Graham)

RESPONSE

Use these questions to share more deeply with each other.

7. List some of the daily pressures you face.

_____

_____

_____

8. How does Jesus' prayer encourage you to face those pressures?

_____

_____

_____

9. What can you learn from this passage about the purpose and practice of prayer?

_____

_____

_____

PRAYER

Father, your Son showed us how to pray. He prayed in the morning, he prayed in the evening, he prayed alone, he prayed with others. In hours of distress he retreated into times of prayer. In hours of joy he lifted his heart to you. Help us to pray in this same way . . . help us to make prayer a priority in our daily lives.

JOURNALING

Take a few moments to record your personal insights from this lesson.

How can I be more involved in the ministry of prayer?

ADDITIONAL QUESTIONS

10. What interferes with your prayer life?

_____

_____

_____

11. How can we overcome feelings of discouragement when our prayers seem to go unanswered?

_____

_____

_____

12. How can prayer affect our lives and the lives of others around us?

_____

_____

_____

For more Bible passages on prayer, see Deuteronomy 4:7; Psalm 32:6; Matthew 14:23; 26:36; Luke 6:28; Ephesians 6:18.

To complete the book of John during this twelve-part study, read John 14:15–17:26.

LESSON ELEVEN

THE RISEN CHRIST

REFLECTION

Begin your study by sharing thoughts on this question.

1. What is the best news you have heard recently? Why was this good news for you?

_____

_____

_____

BIBLE READING

Read John 20:1–18 from the NCV or the NKJV.

NCV

¹Early on the first day of the week, Mary Magdalene went to the tomb while it was still dark. When she saw that the large stone had been moved away from the tomb, ²she ran to Simon Peter and the follower whom Jesus loved. Mary said, "They have taken the Lord out of the tomb, and we don't know where they have put him."

³So Peter and the other follower started for the tomb. ⁴They were both running, but the other follower ran faster than Peter and

NKJV

¹Now on the first day of the week Mary Magdalene went to the tomb early, while it was still dark, and saw that the stone had been taken away from the tomb. ²Then she ran and came to Simon Peter, and to the other disciple, whom Jesus loved, and said to them, "They have taken away the Lord out of the tomb, and we do not know where they have laid Him."

³Peter therefore went out, and the other disciple, and were going to the tomb. ⁴So they both ran together, and the other disciple outran

NCV

reached the tomb first. ⁵He bent down and looked in and saw the strips of linen cloth lying there, but he did not go in. ⁶Then following him, Simon Peter arrived and went into the tomb and saw the strips of linen lying there. ⁷He also saw the cloth that had been around Jesus' head, which was folded up and laid in a different place from the strips of linen. ⁸Then the other follower, who had reached the tomb first, also went in. He saw and believed. ⁹(They did not yet understand from the Scriptures that Jesus must rise from the dead.)

¹⁰Then the followers went back home. ¹¹But Mary stood outside the tomb, crying. As she was crying, she bent down and looked inside the tomb. ¹²She saw two angels dressed in white, sitting where Jesus' body had been, one at the head and one at the feet.

¹³They asked her, "Woman, why are you crying?"

She answered, "They have taken away my Lord, and I don't know where they have put him." ¹⁴When Mary said this, she turned around and saw Jesus standing there, but she did not know it was Jesus.

¹⁵Jesus asked her, "Woman, why are you crying? Whom are you looking for?"

Thinking he was the gardener, she said to him, "Did you take him away, sir? Tell me where you put him, and I will get him."

¹⁶Jesus said to her, "Mary."

Mary turned toward Jesus and said in the Jewish language, "Rabboni." (This means Teacher.)

¹⁷Jesus said to her, "Don't hold on to me, because I have not yet gone up to the Father. But

NKJV

Peter and came to the tomb first. ⁵And he, stooping down and looking in, saw the linen cloths lying there; yet he did not go in. ⁶Then Simon Peter came, following him, and went into the tomb; and he saw the linen cloths lying there, ⁷and the handkerchief that had been around His head, not lying with the linen cloths, but folded together in a place by itself. ⁸Then the other disciple, who came to the tomb first, went in also; and he saw and believed. ⁹For as yet they did not know the Scripture, that He must rise again from the dead. ¹⁰Then the disciples went away again to their own homes.

¹¹But Mary stood outside by the tomb weeping, and as she wept she stooped down and looked into the tomb. ¹²And she saw two angels in white sitting, one at the head and the other at the feet, where the body of Jesus had lain. ¹³Then they said to her, "Woman, why are you weeping?"

She said to them, "Because they have taken away my Lord, and I do not know where they have laid Him."

¹⁴Now when she had said this, she turned around and saw Jesus standing there, and did not know that it was Jesus. ¹⁵Jesus said to her, "Woman, why are you weeping? Whom are you seeking?"

She, supposing Him to be the gardener, said to Him, "Sir, if You have carried Him away, tell me where You have laid Him, and I will take Him away."

¹⁶Jesus said to her, "Mary!"

She turned and said to Him, "Rabboni!" (which is to say, Teacher).

¹⁷Jesus said to her, "Do not cling to Me, for I

NCV	NKJV
go to my brothers and tell them, 'I am going back to my Father and your Father, to my God and your God.'"	have not yet ascended to My Father; but go to My brethren and say to them, 'I am ascending to My Father and your Father, and to My God and your God.'"
[18]Mary Magdalene went and said to the followers, "I saw the Lord!" And she told them what Jesus had said to her.	[18]Mary Magdalene came and told the disciples that she had seen the Lord, and that He had spoken these things to her.

DISCOVERY

Explore the Bible reading by discussing these questions.

2. At what time of day did Mary visit Jesus' tomb? Why do you think she chose that time?

   _____

   _____

   _____

3. How did Mary react when she saw the stone had been moved from the tomb?

   _____

   _____

   _____

4. How did Mary share the good news she received?

   _____

   _____

   _____

5. Based on her actions, how did Mary feel before and after seeing Jesus?

_____

_____

_____

6. How did Jesus' followers respond to the news that his tomb was empty?

_____

_____

_____

INSPIRATION

Here is an uplifting thought from the *Inspirational Study Bible.*

There is something about a living testimony that gives us courage. Once we see someone else emerging from life's dark tunnels we realize that we, too, can overcome.

Could this be why Jesus is called our pioneer? Is this one of the reasons that he consented to enter the horrid chambers of death? It must be. His words, though persuasive, were not enough. His promises, though true, didn't quite allay the fear of the people. His actions, even the act of calling Lazarus from the tomb, didn't convince the crowds that death was nothing to fear. No. In the eyes of humanity, death was still the black veil that separated them from joy. There was no victory over this hooded foe. Its putrid odor invaded the nostrils of every human, convincing them that life was only meant to end abruptly and senselessly.

It was left to the Son of God to disclose the true nature of this force. It was on the cross that the showdown occurred. Christ called for Satan's cards. Weary of seeing humanity fooled by a coverup, he entered the tunnel death to prove that there was indeed an exit. And, as the world darkened, creation held her breath.

Satan threw his best punch, but it wasn't enough. Even the darkness of hell's tunnel was no match for God's Son. Even the chambers of Hades couldn't stop this raider. Legions of screaming demons held nothing over the Lion of Judah.

Christ emerged from death's tunnel, lifted a triumphant fist toward the sky, and freed all from the fear of death.

"Death has been swallowed up in victory!"

(From *On the Anvil*
by Max Lucado)

RESPONSE

Use these questions to share more deeply with each other.

7. Why is Christ's resurrection important for believers?

_____

_____

_____

8. Why do you think it is so hard for some people to believe that Jesus rose from the dead?

_____

_____

_____

9. What does Christ's resurrection mean to you?

_____

_____

_____

PRAYER

Jesus, we thank you for the sweet surprise of Easter morning. We are thankful that when you arose from your sleep of death, you didn't go immediately to heaven, but instead you went and visited people. This visit of love reminds us that it was for people that you died. We praise your name for that sweet surprise.

JOURNALING

Take a few moments to record your personal insights from this lesson.

How can the victory of Christ's resurrection bring victory to my life?

ADDITIONAL QUESTIONS

10. What evidence helps you believe that Jesus rose from the dead?

_____

_____

_____

11. What keeps us from sharing the exciting news of Christ's resurrection with those who don't believe?

_____

_____

_____

12. What objections do people raise about Christ's resurrection? How can we respond to them?

_____

_____

_____

For more Bible passages on the Resurrection, see Matthew 22:31, 32; John 11:25; Acts 1:22; 4:2; 4:33; Romans 1:4; 6:5; 1 Peter 1:3; 3:21.

To complete the book of John during this twelve-part study, read John 18:1–20:18.

ADDITIONAL THOUGHTS

LESSON TWELVE

PETER'S SECOND CHANCE

REFLECTION

Begin your study by sharing thoughts on this question.

1. Think of a time when you helped to restore a broken relationship. How were you able to help in that situation?

_____

_____

_____

BIBLE READING

Read John 21:1–19 from the NCV or the NKJV.

NCV

¹Later, Jesus showed himself to his followers again—this time at Lake Galilee. This is how he showed himself: ²Some of the followers were together: Simon Peter, Thomas (called Didymus), Nathanael from Cana in Galilee, the two sons of Zebedee, and two other followers. ³Simon Peter said, "I am going out to fish."

The others said, "We will go with you." So they went out and got into the boat. They fished that night but caught nothing.

⁴Early the next morning Jesus stood on the

NKJV

¹After these things Jesus showed Himself again to the disciples at the Sea of Tiberias, and in this way He showed Himself: ²Simon Peter, Thomas called the Twin, Nathanael of Cana in Galilee, the sons of Zebedee, and two others of His disciples were together. ³Simon Peter said to them, "I am going fishing."

They said to him, "We are going with you also." They went out and immediately got into the boat, and that night they caught nothing.

⁴But when the morning had now come, Jesus

NCV

shore, but the followers did not know it was Jesus. [5]Then he said to them, "Friends, did you catch any fish?"

They answered, "No."

[6]He said, "Throw your net on the right side of the boat, and you will find some." So they did, and they caught so many fish they could not pull the net back into the boat.

[7]The follower whom Jesus loved said to Peter, "It is the Lord!" When Peter heard him say this, he wrapped his coat around himself. (Peter had taken his clothes off.) Then he jumped into the water. [8]The other followers went to shore in the boat, dragging the net full of fish. They were not very far from shore, only about a hundred yards. [9]When the followers stepped out of the boat and onto the shore, they saw a fire of hot coals. There were fish on the fire, and there was bread.

[10]Then Jesus said, "Bring some of the fish you just caught."

[11]Simon Peter went into the boat and pulled the net to the shore. It was full of big fish, one hundred fifty-three in all, but even though there were so many, the net did not tear. [12]Jesus said to them, "Come and eat." None of the followers dared ask him, "Who are you?" because they knew it was the Lord. [13]Jesus came and took the bread and gave it to them, along with the fish.

[14]This was now the third time Jesus showed himself to his followers after he was raised from the dead.

[15]When they finished eating, Jesus said to Simon Peter, "Simon son of John do you love me more than these?"

NKJV

stood on the shore; yet the disciples did not know that it was Jesus. [5]Then Jesus said to them, "Children, have you any food?"

They answered Him, "No."

[6]And He said to them, "Cast the net on the right side of the boat, and you will find some." So they cast, and now they were not able to draw it in because of the multitude of fish.

[7]Therefore that disciple whom Jesus loved said to Peter, "It is the Lord!" Now when Simon Peter heard that it was the Lord, he put on his outer garment (for he had removed it), and plunged into the sea. [8]But the other disciples came in the little boat (for they were not far from land, but about two hundred cubits), dragging the net with fish. [9]Then, as soon as they had come to land, they saw a fire of coals there, and fish laid on it, and bread. [10]Jesus said to them, "Bring some of the fish which you have just caught."

[11]Simon Peter went up and dragged the net to land, full of large fish, one hundred and fifty-three; and although there were so many, the net was not broken. [12]Jesus said to them, "Come and eat breakfast." Yet none of the disciples dared ask Him, "Who are You?"—knowing that it was the Lord. [13]Jesus then came and took the bread and gave it to them, and likewise the fish.

[14]This is now the third time Jesus showed Himself to His disciples after He was raised from the dead.

[15]So when they had eaten breakfast, Jesus said to Simon Peter, "Simon, son of Jonah, do you love Me more than these?"

He said to Him, "Yes, Lord; You know that I love You."

NCV

He answered, "Yes, Lord, you know that I love you."

Jesus said, "Feed my lambs."

[16]Again Jesus said, "Simon son of John do you love me?"

He answered, "Yes, Lord, you know that I love you."

Jesus said, "Take care of my sheep."

[17]A third time he said, "Simon son of John do you love me?"

Peter was hurt because Jesus asked him the third time, "Do you love me?" Peter said, "Lord, you know everything; you know that I love you!"

He said to him, "Feed my sheep. [18]I tell you the truth, when you were younger, you tied your own belt and went where you wanted. But when you are old, you will put out your hands and someone else will tie you and take you where you don't want to go." [19](Jesus said this to show how Peter would die to give glory to God.) Then Jesus said to Peter, "Follow me!"

NKJV

He said to him, "Feed My lambs."

[16]He said to him again a second time, "Simon, son of Jonah, do you love Me?"

He said to Him, "Yes, Lord; You know that I love You."

He said to him, "Tend My sheep."

[17]He said to him the third time, "Simon, son of Jonah, do you love Me?" Peter was grieved because He said to him the third time, "Do you love Me?"

And he said to Him, "Lord, You know all things; You know that I love You."

Jesus said to him, "Feed My sheep. [18]Most assuredly, I say to you, when you were younger, you girded yourself and walked where you wished; but when you are old, you will stretch out your hands, and another will gird you and carry you where you do not wish." [19]This He spoke, signifying by what death he would glorify God. And when He had spoken this, He said to him, "Follow Me."

DISCOVERY

Explore the Bible reading by discussing these questions.

2. Why did Jesus reveal himself to the disciples in this way?

_____

_____

_____

3. What does Peter's reaction to seeing Jesus reveal about him?

_____

_____

_____

4. How did Jesus restore his relationship with Peter?

_____

_____

_____

5. How did Peter respond to Jesus' words and actions?

_____

_____

_____

6. How did Jesus emphasize the connection between love and service?

_____

_____

_____

INSPIRATION

Here is an uplifting thought from the *Inspirational Study Bible.*

The sun was in the water before Peter noticed it—a wavy circle of gold on the surface of the sea. A fisherman is usually the first to spot the sun rising over the crest of the hills. It means his night of labor is finally over.

But not for this fisherman. Though the light reflected on the lake, the darkness lingered in Peter's heart. The wind chilled, but he didn't feel it. His friends slept soundly, but he didn't care. . . .

His thoughts were far from the Sea of Galilee. His mind was in Jerusalem, reliving an anguished night. As the boat rocked, his memories raced:

the clanking of the Roman guard,

the flash of a sword and the duck of a head,

a touch for Malchus, a rebuke for Peter,

soldiers leading Jesus away.

"What was I thinking?" Peter mumbled to himself as he stared at the bottom of the boat. *Why did I run?*

Peter had run; he had turned his back on his dearest friend and run. We don't know where. Peter may not have known where. He found a hole, a hut, an abandoned shed— he found a place to hide and he hid. . . .

So Peter is in the boat, on the lake. Once again he's fished all night. Once again the sea has surrendered nothing.

His thoughts are interrupted by a shout from the shore. "Catch any fish?" Peter and John look up. Probably a villager. "No!" they yell. "Try the other side!" the voice yells back. John looks at Peter. What harm? So out sails the net.

Peter wraps the rope around his wrist to wait.

But there is no wait. The rope pulls taut and the net catches. Peter sets his weight against the side of the boat and begins to bring in the net; reaching down, pulling up, reaching down, pulling up. He's so intense with the task, he misses the message.

John doesn't. The moment is deja vu. This has happened before. The long night. The empty net. The call to cast again. Fish flapping on the floor of the boat. Wait a minute. He lifts his eyes to the man on the shore. "It's him," he whispers.

Then louder, "It's Jesus."

Then shouting, "It's the Lord, Peter. It's the Lord!"

Peter turns and looks. Jesus has come. Not Jesus the teacher, but Jesus the death-defeater, Jesus King . . . Jesus the victor over darkness. Jesus the God of heaven and earth is on the shore. . . .

Peter plunges into the water, swims to the shore, and stumbles out wet and shivering and stands in front of the friend he betrayed. Jesus has prepared a bed of coals. Both are aware of the last time Peter had stood near a fire. Peter had failed God, but God had come to him.

For one of the few times in his life, Peter is silent. What words would suffice? The moment is too holy for words. God is offering breakfast to the friend who betrayed him. And Peter is once again finding grace at Calvary.

What do you say at a moment like this?

What do *you* say at a moment such as this?

It's just you and God. You and God both know what you did. And neither of you is proud of it. What do you do?

You might consider doing what Peter did. Stand in God's presence. Stand in his sight. Stand still and wait. Sometimes that's all a soul can do. Too repentant to speak, but too hopeful to leave—we just stand.

Stand amazed.
He has come back.
He invites you to try again. This time, with him.

(from *He Still Moves Stones* by Max Lucado)

RESPONSE

Use these questions to share more deeply with each other.

7. What hope does this story offer us?

_____

_____

_____

8. How does this story inspire you to handle your mistakes and failures?

_____

_____

_____

9. When have you experienced God's forgiveness in a meaningful way?

_____

_____

_____

PRAYER

Father, help us as we cope and grapple with yesterday's failures. They weigh us down. Help us to release our regrets to you, Father, and help us to forgive ourselves—even as you have forgiven us—that we might not live burdened and shackled by yesterday's failures, but that we might live free by your grace.

JOURNALING

Take a few moments to record your personal insights from this lesson.

How can I have the depth of compassion for others that Christ has for me?

ADDITIONAL QUESTIONS

10. How can failure destroy a person?

_____

_____

_____

11. What hinders us from accepting and enjoying God's forgiveness?

_____

_____

_____

12. In what failed relationship would you like to experience healing?

_____

_____

_____

For more Bible passages on forgiveness, see Psalm 130:3, 4; Daniel 9:9; Matthew 6:14, 15; Acts 10:43; Ephesians 1:7; Colossians 3:13; 1 John 1:9.

To complete the book of John during this twelve-part study, read John 20:19–21:25.

ADDITIONAL THOUGHTS

LEADERS' NOTES

LESSON ONE

Question 2: In preparation, you may want to study some of the prophecies about the Messiah. Jesus' birth and life fulfilled all Old Testament prophecies regarding the Messiah. (1) Micah 5:2 is fulfilled in Matthew 2:1–6; (2) Isaiah 7:14 is fulfilled in Luke 1:26–38; (3) Psalm 22:14–17 is fulfilled in Mark 15:20, 25; (4) Isaiah 53:5–12 is fulfilled in John 1:29; 11:49–52.

Question 7: You may find people have many questions about the mystery of the incarnation. The group may want to look up some of the following verses and read them together: Matthew 16:27; John 1:14; 10:37–38; 14:7–13; 17:22; Colossians 2:9; Hebrews 1:1–3.

LESSON TWO

Question 4: Obviously, this miracle saved a bride and groom from embarrassment. But the ultimate reason for this miracle is found in John 2:11.

LESSON THREE

Question 1: If the members of your group have not already shared their testimonies with each other, this will be a good opportunity to get to know one another better. Plan extra time for sharing and listening to everyone's stories.

Question 2: The details of this story reveal a lot about the reputation of the woman at the well. Unlike most women, who drew water in the morning and evening, this woman drew her water in the heat of the day, probably to avoid the condescending glares of the townspeople. She had five husbands and was living in sin with another man who was not her husband. Jesus looked past her bad reputation and saw a needy person.

Question 7: Some people may feel uncomfortable identifying with a morally corrupt woman who was shunned by her community. Be prepared to share your answer first. Also suggest some things all people have in common with this woman (i.e., we've all made mistakes we're ashamed of, we all need God's forgiveness, etc.).

Question 8: The following verses tell us more about God's attitude toward sinners: Luke 15:7; Matthew 9:12–13; Romans 5:8; 1 Timothy 1:15.

LESSON FOUR

Question 2: You may want to explain that people believed that the springs at this pool in Bethesda held healing powers. The sick laid on the steps descending into the pool hoping to receive healing from the water.

Question 6: Take some time to read other passages of Jesus healing the sick: Matthew 4:23–24; 8:3; 12:22–23; 14:35–36; 21:14; Mark 1:30–31; 10:46–52; Luke 13:10–13; 17:11–14. Jesus' extensive ministry to suffering people reveals his compassion, sensitivity, mercy, and love.

LESSON FIVE

The story of Jesus feeding the five thousand is also found in Matthew 14:13–21, Mark 6:30–44, and Luke 9:10–17.

Question 4: In Philip's mind, eight month's wages was too much money to spend on lunch for a crowd of strangers. Jesus wanted Philip to realize that it was humanly impossible for them to feed the crowd—they needed a miracle! Sometimes we must come to the same realization.

LESSON SIX

Question 2: The religious leaders' actions followed the letter of the law. The woman deserved to be stoned to death for her sin. See Leviticus 20:10 and Deuteronomy 22:22. Jesus taught them a lesson on the spirit of the law.

LESSON SEVEN

Questions 2 and 3: People in Jewish culture made a connection between a person's illness and his or her moral character. They assumed sick people were guilty of great sins and were somewhat responsible for their condition. Jesus corrected this misguided notion, challenging people to show compassion rather than pass judgment.

Question 5: Hezekiah built a 1770-foot underground tunnel that carried water from a spring outside the city into the pool of Siloam. People believed this pool was a sacred place, similar to the pool at Bethesda.

Question 7: If you have a large group, you may want to divide into smaller groups. Ask one group to study the blind man's response to Jesus and the other to discuss the reaction of the townspeople. Ask each group to prepare a list of principles we can learn from each person(s) response.

LESSON EIGHT

Question 2: To learn more about Mary and Martha's relationship with Jesus, read Mark 14:3–9; Luke 10:38–42; and John 11:1–3; 12:1–3.

Question 7: Follow up with this question: What lessons can we learn from Martha's example?

LESSON NINE

This lesson looks at Jesus' last celebration of the Passover with his disciples. Passover is a Jewish feast that celebrates Israel's exodus from Egypt. To learn more about it, read Exodus 12:1–50; Leviticus 23:4, 5; Numbers 9:4, 5; Luke 2:41, 42.

Question 5: Keep in mind that washing the guest's feet was a menial job, saved for the lowest household servants.

Question 9: When the immediate rewards don't motivate us to serve, we can remind ourselves of the eternal rewards: Matthew 25:21; John 12:26; Romans 14:18; Ephesians 6:7, 8; Colossians 3:23, 24; 1 Timothy 3:13.

LESSON TEN

Question 4: Jesus asked the Father to sanctify his followers. God sanctifies us by cleansing us from sin, making us holy, and setting us apart for his use. We become involved in the process by reading and obeying God's Word (2 Timothy 3:16; Hebrews 4:12).

Questions 5 and 6: To learn more about spiritual warfare, read 2 Corinthians 10:3–5; 1 Peter 2:11; and Ephesians 6:10–18.

LESSON ELEVEN

The story of Jesus' appearance to Mary Magdalene is also found in Matthew 28:1–10; Mark 16:1–13; and Luke 24:1–12. Mary was a devoted follower of Jesus since he had driven seven demons out of her. She showed her gratitude by being with Jesus at the cross and visiting his tomb. After Jesus' resurrection, Mary was the first person to whom he appeared. Mary is also mentioned in Matthew 27:56; Mark 15:47; Luke 8:2.

Question 7: Discuss why Jesus' resurrection is the key to our faith. See 1 Corinthians 15:12–19.

LESSON TWELVE

Question 2: Luke 5:1–11 records a similar miracle performed by Jesus.

Question 4: Because of his humiliating failure in the preceding days, Peter desperately needed Jesus' forgiveness, reassurance, and love. Jesus offered that and more—he commissioned Peter for future ministry.

ADDITIONAL NOTES

ADDITIONAL NOTES

ADDITIONAL NOTES

ADDITIONAL NOTES

ACKNOWLEDGMENTS

Graham, Billy. *Hope for the Troubled Heart*, copyright 1991, W Publishing Group, Nashville, TN.

Lucado, Max. *The Applause of Heaven*, copyright 1990, W Publishing Group, Nashville, TN.

Lucado, Max. *God Came Near*, Questar Publishers, Multnomah Books, copyright 1987.

Lucado, Max. *He Still Moves Stones*, copyright 1993, W Publishing Group, Nashville, TN.

Lucado, Max. *In the Eye of the Storm*, copyright 1991, W Publishing Group, Nashville, TN.

Lucado, Max. *On the Anvil*, copyright 1985 by Max Lucado. Used by permission of Tyndale House Publishers, Inc. All rights reserved.

Lucado, Max. *Six Hours One Friday*, Questar Publishers, Multnomah Books, copyright 1989 by Max Lucado.

Lucado, Max. *When God Whispers Your Name*, copyright 1994, W Publishing Group, Nashville, TN.

Ortlund, Anne. *Discipling One Another*, copyright 1979 W Publishing Group, Nashville, TN.